The Seedbed of Pakistan

Cultural Conflicts, Elite Muslim Anxieties, and the Congress

1885-1906

Saumya Dey

Vitasta

To

The feet of my Iṣta, Prabhu Anjaneya.

For the Sylheti-Hindu victims of Partition.

Published by
Renu Kaul Verma
Vitasta Publishing Pvt Ltd
2/15, Ansari Road, Daryaganj
New Delhi – 110 002
info@vitastapublishing.com

ISBN 978-93-90961-89-4

First Edition 2023
MRP ₹525

Edited by Anuradha Mukherjee
Cover and layout by Somesh Kumar Mishra
Printed by Vikas Computer and Printers

CONTENTS

ACKNOWLEDGEMENTS

I owe an immense intellectual debt to Prof. Bhagwan Josh, former faculty at the Center for Historical Studies, Jawaharlal Nehru University. I originally acquired the outlines of several ideas developed in the second and third chapters of this book while writing my MPhil dissertation under his supervision. I owe my sincerest thanks to Dr Ravi K Mishra, Deputy Director, Nehru Memorial Museum and Library (NMML), for permitting me to incorporate a rewritten and modified version of the paper 'Forging the Nation: The Congress Demand for Representative Bodies and Elite Muslim Anxieties. 1885-1892' into the fourth chapter of this book. It was originally published by NMML in its 'Occasional Papers' series. I am grateful to Prof. Salil Misra, faculty at the School of Liberal Studies, Ambedkar University, who read an early draft of 'Forging the Nation' and enriched it with his criticism and suggestions. I am greatly obliged to the staff of the National Archives of India and NMML, and Mr Sunil Kumar, late librarian at the Center for Historical

Studies, Jawaharlal Nehru University. My research work was eased at every step by their kindness and alacrity in rendering assistance. Finally, I am limitlessly grateful to Mr Shobhit Mathur and Mr Sahil Aggarwal, Vice Chancellor and CEO, Rishihood University. I could not have brought this project to its conclusion without their precious and ever-present support. Thanks for always backing this struggling author.

INTRODUCTION

BRITISH-RULED INDIA was partitioned into the two Dominions of India and Pakistan in 1947. This cataclysm displaced enormous numbers of human beings. Millions of Hindus, Sikhs, and Muslims found themselves on the wrong side of a hurriedly etched international border and trudged to safety in India or Pakistan. Simultaneously, hundreds of thousands died in the sanguinary riots that backdropped partition—old neighbours fell upon and slaughtered each other in savage, bestial fury in many cities and countless towns and villages. Although three generations have passed since this monstrous human tragedy unfolded, its traumatic memories are yet to fade. We still, as a result, look for the roots of this tragedy. We continue to search for what might have led to partition and the emergence of Pakistan in the political bedlam that characterised India in the 1930s and 40s. More specifically, we look to pin the blame for the enormous cataclysm that was partition on some cogent reason or identifiable agency.

Now, most important scholarship agrees that the Congress stood for Indian unity throughout[1] (though one might personally want to nurture a different point of view). Scholarly speculations, thus, generally revolve around Muhammad Ali Jinnah's role and intentions in the political drama surrounding partition. Ayesha Jalal seems to think that he did not quite want Pakistan and meant it only as a 'bargaining counter'.[2] Anita Inder Singh, on the other hand, appears to indicate that Jinnah did after all want partition and the establishment of Pakistan.[3] It is indeed tempting to engage with and contribute to these speculations and points of view, as it gives one the chance to contemplate and dilate on the sensational course of developments leading to the blood-drenched sundering of British India. This book shall, however, not do so, as is clearly indicated by the period it considers. Instead, the intention of this relatively brief narrative is to examine what might be termed the discursive foundations of the Pakistan idea in the way of certain tendencies, psychologies, perspectives, and political manoeuvres discernible over the late nineteenth and early twentieth centuries as a nascent Congress tried to

---

1 Sekhar Bandyopadhyay, *From Plassey to Partition and After. A History of Modern India* (Hyderabad: Orient BlackSwan, 2022 [Second Edition]), p.461.

2 See *The Sole Spokesman. Jinnah, the Muslim League and the Demand for Pakistan* (CUP, 2017).

3 See *The Origins of the Partition of India. 1936-47* (Bombay, Calcutta, Madras: OUP, 1990).

overcome the opposition of some upper-class Muslims along with indifference from Muslims at large. This book shall survey, one might say, the seedbed of Pakistan. This is so that we may acquire a rather fresh and more nuanced understanding of the late colonial politics that eventually resulted in its creation.

An unmistakable fact about colonial India is that the elite segment of Indian Muslim society, namely, the *ashrāf*, largely chose to plough their own political furrows. Leading members of *ashrāf* society, as we shall see, staunchly opposed the Congress after it was founded in 1885. Syed Ahmed Khan, for instance, supported neither the Congress's imagination of Indian nationhood nor the political reforms demanded by it. Eventually, in 1906, a number of the *ashrāf* approached the colonial establishment and demanded that it grant the Indian Muslims proportional representation on a communal basis. In other words, these Indo-Muslim elites (as we shall term the *ashrāf*), sought to establish Indian Muslims as a distinct political interest group deserving of special consideration. Styling themselves the 'Simla Deputation,' these gentlemen even termed the Indian Muslims a 'nation' as they met with Lord Minto in the summer capital of British India. Exactly three months after they did, the All-India Muslim League (AIML) was founded in Dhaka, again by prominent Indo-Muslim elites. The AIML, we might say, was but an organisational expression of the Simla Deputation's points of view in the long term. It sought to champion the ostensibly distinct political interests of Indian Muslims and eventually, in 1940, argued that they, being a nation in their own right, ought to have their own territorial state. In little over seven years after the 'Lahore Resolution' was passed by the AIML, Pakistan was a reality.

Why did the Indo-Muslim elite keep aloof from the Congress's articulation of Indian nationhood as well as its political programme? Going by what some influential scholarship has to say, it might seem that it was largely due to how the colonial state stood in relation to a generally backward Indian Muslim society. For instance, as Peter Hardy puts it, Indian Muslims acquired a 'separate social as well as religious personality'[4] when the British rulers sought to address their backwardness in education. Hardy suggests that they did so after becoming very conscious of the Indian Muslims, 'sometimes as a ghoul, sometimes as a phantom, sometimes as a Frankenstein's monster, but always as a bogy'.[5] Apparently, while the British were intervening as 'a colonial power in the centre of the Muslim world,'[6] the seemingly extra-territorial loyalties of the Indian Muslims were causing them concern. The upper strata of Indian Muslims, on their part, responded to the colonial state's willingness to accommodate Muslim interests. As Hardy writes,

> A perceptive Muslim of the educated classes could see in the eighteen-seventies and early eighties that the British were ready to treat Muslims as a distinct political interest in India.[7]

4 Peter Hardy, *The Muslims of British India* (CUP, 1998), p.122.
5 Ibid., p.118.
6 Ibid.
7 Ibid., p.125.

Mushirul Hasan, on the other hand, appears to think that Muslims mobilised as a distinct political interest group in India because the colonial state *did not* cater to them through patronage and dispersal of resources. As he puts it, a 'separate and distinct political consciousness' among Indian Muslims was caused by their placement 'in the political and economic structures and their access to the levers of power, authority, and influence under colonial rule'. That is why, he says, 'communal antipathy' was the greatest in Bengal since 'Muslims had virtually no access to the resources of the province'[8]. Thus, in effect, like Hardy, Hasan too argues that at the root of Indian Muslim politics lay backwardness. It is only that he arrives at this argument through a different route. M. Mujeeb, author of a classic and exhaustive study titled *The Indian Muslims*, appears to be on the same page as Hardy and Hasan. The realisation of being 'backward subjects of a non-Muslim state'[9] was the reason why, Mujeeb seemingly insinuates, the Indian Muslims developed their own unique political point of view.

The contentions of Hardy, Hasan, and Mujeeb might seem compelling at first glance, but are exposed to be rather ill-founded on closer scrutiny. The Indo-Muslim elites, or the *ashrāf,* who were at the helm of Muslim politics in colonial India were anything but backward, nor did they generally base their politics on the educational or economic laggardness of

---

8 Mushirul Hasan, *Nationalism and Communal Politics in India, 1885-1930* (New Delhi: Manohar, 2000), p.13.

9 M. Mujeeb, *The Indian Muslims* (New Delhi: Munshiram Manoharlal Publishers Pvt. Ltd., 2017 [Fourth Reprint]), p.528.

Muslims. Francis Robinson, as a matter of fact, points out how Muslims were a rather dominant minority in the United Provinces, disproportionately well represented in both land ownership and government jobs. In his schema, this class of Muslims began to politically organise as there was an *erosion* of their erstwhile status in the province. For example, he writes that the colonial administration's attempts to introduce western learning and promote vernaculars 'threatened' their 'religious beliefs, social customs and political position'. Simultaneously, bureaucratic reforms reduced this elite's power and the introduction of elective principle in local government 'undermined its influence'.[10]

Based on what Francis Robison says, one is tempted to think that the politics of the Indo-Muslim elite might have been motivated by cultural concerns and distrust of representative democracy. This is probably why, as Farzana Shaikh observes, the *ashrāf* brought a very culturally derived language to their politics which was meant to establish how 'special' they were, regardless of numbers. As it seems, this might be because they had once formed the apex of the 'ruling class structure,' which had made some 'Mongol-Mughal' ideas a part of their political thinking. Also, Shaikh thinks that some of the *ashrāf* political psychology was 'Islamically-derived' and drew upon 'assumptions familiar to Muslim political discourse since the

10 Francis Robinson, *Separatism Among Indian Muslims. The Politics of the United Provinces' Muslims. 1860*-1923 (New Delhi: OUP, 1994 [Second Impression]), p.34.

consolidation of Islam as a world religion'.[11] The substantive implication of Shaikh's observations, from our point of view, is that an examination of *ashrāf* politics must factor in their Mughal heritage as well as a moral imagination that issued from Islam. Let this be the note on which we commence our narrative.

As a society, the Indo-Muslim elite had been brought forth by the Mughal Empire and, one may contend, represented its cultural discourse. Every state has a cultural persona, or, rather, as this book shall argue, states are culture-power formations—they project and broadcast power through cultural symbols or tropes. The cultural persona of the Mughal Empire, it is contended in this study, was 'Islamicate'—it projected power using cultural tropes and symbols broadly associable with Muslims as a society. These were, to begin with, a moral discourse derived from Islam, the Persian language, and association with Sufi holy men. Curtailment of the cultural displays of non-Muslims was also an aspect of the 'Islamicate' cultural persona of the Mughal Empire. The *ashrāf* formed the bureaucratic vanguard of the Islamicate culture-power formation that was the Mughal Empire. They, thus, represented the 'Islamicate' cultural paradigm as a society—both the moral discourse of Islam and Sufi spirituality were reflected in their lives, and they displayed a strong preference for Persian and the 'Persianate'

11 Farzana Sheikh, *Community and Consensus in Islam. Muslim representation in Colonial India. 1860-1947* (Melbourne: CUP, 1989), p.79.

tongue of Urdu; they might also, in association with non-elite Muslims, curtail the cultural displays of non-Muslims. The *ashrāf* dominated the little, semi-urban settlements in the Gangetic heartland, or *qasbās*, and lent them a broadly 'Islamicate' cultural appearance.

With the onset of the nineteenth century, we see that the *ashrāf*, or the Indo-Muslim elite, are finding the going rather difficult as both administrators and land controllers. Simultaneously, we notice the ascendent Hindu elites getting assertive in the urban spaces that the *ashrāf* had formerly administered or dominated. There are also outbreaks of Hindu-Muslim strife. There is, thus, a relative decline in the temporal status of the *ashrāf*—the Indo-Muslim elite are ceasing to be a dominant minority. The open disregard for their way of life that the new rulers showed, however, is likely to have distressed them more; the British did not hold much concern for the cultural graces that distinguished the Indo-Muslim elite. An initial response to the emotional anguish that Indo-Muslim elite society was undergoing came from the *ulāmā*, an important component thereof. This is understandable, since, Indian Islam was without courtly patronage under the new political dispensation. The *ulāmā* themselves, on the other hand, were gradually denied a role in the functioning of the colonial state. In this situation, they took it upon themselves to protect and nurture the Islamic heritage of India. The *ulāmā* launched into reform efforts that left Indian Islam quite transformed. By abolishing a slew of local cultural practices, the reformist *ulāmā*, in a way, reengineered Indian Muslim society and rendered it more culturally and politically cohesive. These reform efforts made the elite and non-elite Indian Muslims come together.

In the process, we might say, the Indo-Muslim elite acquired a conspicuous leadership role in broader Indian Muslim society. Alongside, the Indo-Muslim elite were in search of their own iteration of modernity. This quest first expressed itself as the hybrid seminary at Deoband—it was very likely inspired by the Delhi College established by the colonial administration and was an institution somewhat in the Western mould. Later, the Indo-Muslim elite set about acquiring a more obviously Western-inspired modernity at the Muhammadan Anglo-Oriental College. Founded in Aligarh in 1875, this brainchild of Syed Ahmed Khan, a prominent *sharif*, was meant to regenerate Indian Muslim society at large and reconcile it with Western reason and British rule. At this historical juncture, with the *ashrāf* very delicately poised, the 'Islamicate' cultural tropes cherished by them came under vigorous assault. For instance, the British unseated the Persian language as a medium of court proceedings. The Hindus of the Gangetic heartland, on the other hand, waged extremely aggressive agitations promoting Hindi-Nagari against Urdu and regulations for cow protection. They wanted Hindi written in the Devanagari script to be granted an official position equivalent to Urdu and sought to keep Muslims from sacrificing cows on Bakr Id by resorting to violence. Further, Hindus were achieving trans-local solidarity as a society, or 'communitas,' by conducting their public religious ceremonials with greater verve. In the process, the 'Islamicate' ambience of the *qasbās* became hard to sustain for the Indo-Muslim elite. There was, in other words, a proper cultural conflict underway in North India at this historical turn, with Hindus deploying and asserting their cultural symbols against the Indian Muslim society. This cultural conflict was exacerbated by the introduction of local self-government. Due to their advantage in numbers, Hindus were more successful in municipal politics than Muslims. They would gain control of the local boards and, often, seek to implement their cultural agendas. The franchise and representative institutions, thus, were further imperilling the 'Islamicate' cultural paradigm which had once been hegemonic in the urban spaces of North India.

The Indian National Congress was established against the backdrop of intensifying cultural conflicts and Hindu assertion in colonial North India. It arrived on the scene with a somewhat unstable conception of Indian nationhood and demands for, what seemed to its detractors, radical political reforms. The Congress visualised the Indian nation as a purely civic entity while also implying that it is a federation of religious and normative groups which are internally autonomous in terms of values and mores. We see that the Congress refused to discuss matters of social reform so as to realise its imagination of the Indian nation; as an expedient measure, it restricted itself to the political issues that were supposedly relevant to all its constituents. This meant that it was an option for groups or individuals to refuse to be counted in this Indian nation of the Congress's imagination. We see that that is precisely what happened. The Congress found it hard to explain the relatively small numbers of Muslim delegates at its annual sessions. It seemed like Muslims were unwilling to join the Indian nation that the Congress had meant to bring forth. And, then, prominent *ashrāf*, or Indo-Muslim elites, such as Nawab Abdul Latif, Syed Ameer Ali, and Syed Ahmed Khan all dissed the Congress. Khan, in particular, emphatically denied that India could claim to be a nation as he corresponded with Badruddin Tyabji, a lawyer from Bombay who had presided over the annual Congress session in 1887. These *ashrāf* were all wary of the Congress since it demanded franchise-based representative bodies at the provincial and central levels of British India—Syed Ahmed Khan termed this 'monstrous' and 'unreasonable'. He feared that the introduction of the vote and representative institutions in the country would put Muslims completely at the mercy of the Hindu majority since the latter four times outnumbered the former. The *Aligarh Institute Gazette*, very likely taking its editorial cue from him, was pretty blunt in stating that Hindus might use the franchise and their domination of an Indian parliament to re-introduce Sati and ban cow slaughter. The Indo-Muslim elite were visibly anxious on account of the Congress's political programme, clearly deriving this anxiety from the cultural conflicts that were underway and Muslims' experience with local-level politics. After some initial inactivity, the Congress made multiple manoeuvres to soothe this anxiety and bring around the Indo-Muslim elite. Badruddin Tyabji corresponded with Khan and Syed Ameer Ali at various points in 1887 and 1888 and urged them to come over to Congress with their unique Muslim point of view. They did not listen. Later, convening in Allahabad, the Congress institutionalised communal vetoes through a resolution that laid down that it would not take up any matter for discussion to which the Hindu or Muslim delegates objected—the move was Tyabji's brainchild. The Congress also accepted proportional representation for religious groups in principle at its 1889 annual session. While it did, Muslims from its own ranks rose to demand first parity and then weightage for Indian Muslims in political representation. Over the 1890s, Muslim participation in the Congress plummeted. On the other hand, Congress ceased to engage with the anxieties of the Indo-Muslim elite. It even unilaterally termed itself the sole representative of the Indian nation. Things did not change in the next century. Muslims continued to avoid the Congress, perhaps because it now demanded representative bodies on an elective basis with greater confidence and urgency. The colonial state finally showed a willingness to consider this demand in 1906. As this became known, Nawab Muhsin-ul-Mulk, the Secretary of the Muhammadan Anglo-Oriental College at Aligarh, arranged for a Muslim delegation to be received by Lord Minto. It has gone down in history as the 'Simla Deputation'. This was a historical instant when the anxieties of the Indo-Muslim elite went mainstream in the politics of colonial India. The immediate outcome of this mainstreaming was the AIML, while the staggered outcomes, as this book shall argue, were the 'Lahore Resolution' and the state of Pakistan.

THE MUGHAL EMPIRE AND THE INDO-MUSLIM ELITE
THE 'ISLAMICATE' LEGACY

STATES 'WEAR' A CULTURE

STATES HAVE A cultural persona. Or, one could say that they 'wear' culture just as we human beings wear garments. The cultural aspect of states could be discerned in the arena of geopolitics and international relations since it seems to bear the potential of determining their dynamics. Apparently, states belonging to the same cultural sphere could gravitate towards each other and have the same friends and foes. As the controversial political scientist Samuel P. Huntington writes, 'Cultural commonalities and differences shape the interests, antagonism, and associations of states'.[1] Thus, he

1 *The Clash of Civilizations and the Remaking of World Order* (Penguin Books, 2016), p.29.

argues, the Western countries formed NATO as their 'central security organisation' on account of their 'common values and philosophical assumptions'. The European Union, on the other hand, 'is the product of a common European culture'.[2] The cultural persona of states sometimes becomes extremely obvious when they choose a side during an outbreak of international military conflict. According to Huntington, 'Muslims everywhere rallied against' the Soviet Union when it intervened in Afghanistan since in their eyes it was a 'civilisational war'.[3] Though he does not elaborate as to how the Soviet intervention in Afghanistan was a civilizational war, it seems safe to assume that Muslim countries saw it as an instance of a godless communist state battling True Belief.

This chapter seeks to argue that the Mughal Empire manifested a cultural persona that can be termed 'Islamicate'. Further, it will contend that this 'Islamicate' persona shaped the Indo-Muslim elite since they inhabited the cultural spaces that it created, and inherited the cultural forms and practices that constituted it. However, before we can advance these arguments, we must understand what 'state' and 'culture' actually are. Once we have done this, we shall take a historical overview of the relationship between the two, both in the European and Indian contexts, in order to develop some sense of the various forms and functionalities it assumed. These

2 Ibid., p.131.
3 Ibid., p.247.

exercises will help us contextualise and better understand the Mughal Empire as an 'Islamicate' state form and how the Indo-Muslim elite stood in relation to it.

UNDERSTANDING STATE AND CULTURE

How does one define the state? Though the question has generated an enormous amount of theoretical literature, we think a simple answer to it is possible. One could call the state the ultimate 'order enforcing authority'. In the words of the social anthropologist Ernest Gellner, the state 'is that institution or set of institutions specifically concerned with the maintenance of order'. Examples of the latter would be the police force and courts. According to Gellner, the state comes into existence when these institutions have attained autonomy and 'separate out from the rest of social life'.[4] Thus, the state is those agencies which keep our persons and property safe and ensure that mobs do not (normally) riot in the streets. It is the state on account of which we have the confidence of returning alive when we step out of our homes to earn a livelihood in the morning. Our hunter gatherer ancestors, living in an age when neither the policeman nor the magistrate existed, almost certainly lacked this confidence when leaving their caves to find nourishment. Quarrelling over an antelope's leg or a bunch of berries, one caveman or woman could always brain

4 Ernest Gellner, *Nations and Nationalism* (Ithaca, New York: Cornell University Press, 2006), p.4.

another. But what is it exactly that makes the state capable of enforcing order? Well, it is power. The courts and policemen enjoy legitimate power over us, do they not? That is how they protect us. So, we could term the state, on account of its order-enforcing role, the systematic and institutionalised application of power. The state is 'a territorial society' which enjoys 'within its allotted physical area, a supremacy over all other institutions'.[5] In other words, we could say that the state is that power which is (in an ideal situation) final and incontrovertible within a delimited territory and upon a social body—a mass of human beings—and all forms of association that comprise it.

What is culture then? To answer this question, let us resort to the very influential observations of the famous anthropologist Clifford Geertz. He espouses a 'semiotic' conception of culture.[6] In simple language, Geertz thinks that cultures are complexes of symbols. These symbols are both extremely potent and conspicuous. They are 'a set of control mechanisms—plans, recipes, rules, instructions' for the governing of behaviour.[7] Their 'natural habitat is the house yard, the marketplace, and the town square'.[8] 'Culture is public,' writes Geertz, 'because meaning is'.[9] Apparently, we are to understand culture as these meaning producing symbols that are all around; culture

5 A. Appadorai, *The Substance of Politics* (New Delhi: OUP, 2020 [Twenty-Seventh Impression]), p.13.

6 Clifford Geertz, *The Interpretation of Cultures* (New York: Basic Books, 1973), p.5.

7 Ibid., p.44.

8 Ibid., p.45.

9 Ibid., p.12.

is what is evocative and conspicuous. But how exactly does it govern our behaviour? Geertz says that it does so by organising our thinking as 'traffic' in 'significant symbols'.[10] We could build on this remark by Geertz and say that culture is sacred insignias such as the crescent, the cross, or the sacred syllable 'Om,' that it is sacred books, shrines, deities, sacred sites, ritual performances, and forms of behaviour with meanings encoded into them. Culture is an entire range of evocative symbols which might frame and organise our psychology and from which we might derive thoughts and ideas. This is how cultures are 'set[s] of symbolic devices for controlling human behaviour' and 'historically created systems of meaning in terms of which we give form, order, point and direction to our lives'.[11]

The range of evocative symbols mentioned above, for example, is always animate with a large mass of historically accumulated meanings. They can shape life choices and extract the staunchest allegiance from human beings. And, finally, culture is socially reproduced. From the point of view of an individual the symbols that constitute it 'are largely given,' and s/he finds them 'already current in the community when [s/he] is born…'[12] So, we could end by terming culture a socially inherited habitus of meanings induced by symbols that regulate and lend purpose to human behaviour and actions. That is why, culture can be, and usually is, such an effective

10 Ibid.

11 Ibid., p.52.

12 Ibid.

instrument for power, for the state. After all, states too are in the business of regulating and directing human behaviour and actions in a social context.

THE INTERACTION OF STATE AND CULTURE. INSTANCES FROM EUROPE AND INDIA

Historically, European states have acquired cultural personas through their espousal of a language or religion. This is understandable, since language and religion have been termed the 'central elements of any culture or civilization'.[13] As we see, the former is the means through which we express meanings, while the latter is the repository of symbols furnishing meanings. The modern European nation-state largely originated through identification with a language, or it emerged as a standardised language that became the speech of a 'national community'. How and why did this happen? There are some famous scholarly explanations.

According to the historian Eric Hobsbawm, European states were democratised in the nineteenth century and turned their subjects into citizens. Then warfare came to be such that it required the large-scale participation of ordinary people. As a result, European states had to perforce identify with the populations they ruled and seek legitimacy among them. Partly, they sought to do this by utilising sentiments and symbols. European states, thus, 'invented traditions' (the national anthem being an example) to elicit the emotional allegiance of

---

13 *The Clash of Civilizations*, p.59.

the populations they ruled. Secondly, they attached themselves to a particular 'national language,' that is, they tried to become the 'national states' of certain linguistic groups. However, since these states were generally quite heterogeneous, the adoption of a 'national language' inevitably left parts of their populations, which did not speak it, alienated. This caused a proliferation of nationalisms and nation states as multiple linguistic groups of Europe now tried to acquire their own states.[14]

According to Ernest Gellner, the congruence between states and linguistic communities is a post-industrial phenomenon. Prior to the advent of the industrial age, agrarian societies were culturally fragmented and heterogeneous as they lacked mass literacy and, consequently, linguistic homogeneity. A privileged few monopolized literacy in these societies and most of their populations were divided into culturally differentiated small communities. There was, thus, no linguistic cohesion between the elite and non-elite and even among the non-elite.[15] Resultantly, the typical political unit in the agrarian age was one in which a 'central dominant authority' co-existed with 'semi-autonomous local units'.[16] The fusion between polity and culture happened in the industrial age, because an industrial society required standardised mass literacy so that

14 Eric Hobsbawm, *Nations and Nationalism since 1780* (CUP, 2012 [Second Edition]). See Chapter 3, 'The Government Perspective' and Chapter 4, 'The Transformation of Nationalism, 1870-1918'.

15 *Nations and Nationalism* (Ithaca, New York: Cornell University Press, 2006), pp.9-10.

16 Ibid., p.14.

individuals were mobile, not restricted to their traditional roles, and (theoretically) anyone at a job was replaceable by anyone. This caused the erasure of the linguistic diversity characteristic of agrarian societies as industrializing states built a national education system in which everyone was socialised, taught, and trained the same way. The result was that, according to Gellner, industrialised states identified themselves with a particular language and culture and turned into national states. They also, he contends, created nations in the process.[17]

According to the political scientist Benedict Anderson, the linguistic nation-state (which he termed an imagined political community) emerged in Europe in the wake of print capitalism—the invention of the printing press that made possible the publishing industry. A catalyst in the process was the Reformation (beginning in 1518). As Martin Luther (1483-1546) polemicized against the Catholic Church, 'a religious propaganda war' broke out in Europe. Continuing into the next century, it created a vernacular print market. Martin Luther's writings, for example, were brought out in cheap popular editions and created 'large, new reading publics'.[18] Apparently, as more and more people now read the same stuff in the vernaculars they spoke everyday (German, English, French, Spanish, etc), they were connected to each other in 'unified fields of exchange and communication'.[19] This, according to Anderson, provided a basis for national consciousness.

---

17 See Chapter 3, 'Industrial Society'.

18 *Imagined Communities* (London, New York: Verso, 2006), p.40.

19 Ibid., p.44.

Much later, in the nineteenth century, printing technology facilitated a large quantum of pioneering lexicographical and grammatical work. Dictionaries and grammars of hitherto marginal languages such as Ukrainian and Norwegian were now composed and published. The result was the growth of multiple new linguistic nationalisms.[20]

As is demonstrated by Hobsbawm, Gellner, and Anderson, the linguistic nation-state in Europe is of relatively recent historical vintage. We learn that the modern alliance between state forms and languages might have occurred as the former sought to fulfil certain instrumentalities related to governmentality[21] and the industrial economy. Or this alliance might be the outcome of the tremendous boost to communication and, consequently, the 'national consciousness' given by printing technology. Irrespective of the precise historical circumstances that occasioned the European style linguistic nation-state, it is doubtless that a standardised state sponsored language serves as a conduit for state power (think of the ease of surveillance when all citizens use the same language), or it legitimises this power among the citizenry by generating

20 See Chapter 5, 'Old Languages, New Models'.

21 A term coined by the French philosopher Michel Foucault. As explained by him, it broadly denotes the 'institutions, procedures, analyses, and reflections' through which a 'complex form of power' is exercised upon a population. Governmentality involves the 'formation of a whole series of specific government apparatuses' as well as a 'whole complex of knowledge'. It is about the emergence and 'governmentalization' of the 'administrative state.'
See Michel Foucault, *Power. Essential Works. 1954-84. Volume Three* (Penguin Random House, 1994), pp.219-220.

a sense of belonging to the same civic, political community ('national consciousness'). The modern linguistic nation-state, thus, enforces or buttresses its power by allying with a language.

In the centuries before the linguistic nation-state came into existence, premodern European states exhibited a cultural persona primarily by patronising religion—always a rich purveyor of symbols in the form of deities, shrines, and sacred texts. Typically, they made a visible, public demonstration of their support for religion by investing in monumental sacred architecture. Take for instance the building projects of Augustus, the first Roman Emperor (r. 27 BCE-14 CE). They were both numerous and very ambitious, as we learn from his autobiography, *Res Gestae Divi Augusti*. Augustus constructed the Senate House, restored the Capitol and Theatre of Pompey, and completed the Forum Julium.[22] But he also, spent copiously on the shrines of deities. 'I restored,' Augustus declares in the *Res Gestae*, 'eighty-two temples of the gods on the authority of the Senate, neglecting none that required restoration at that time…I built the temple of Mars the Avenger [Mars Ultor]…'[23] The wealth lavished on these shrines by Augustus could be due to his personal piety, we do not dismiss this likelihood. However, since the Roman state was effectively coincident with the person of the Emperor, Augustus restoring and building temples doubtless implied a grand display of the support

---

22 See Colin Wells, *The Roman Empire* (Fontana Press, 1992 [Second Edition]), p.79.

23 Ibid., pp.79-80.

lent to the Roman religion by the Roman state. Later, when the Roman Empire renounced paganism for Christianity, it exhibited a religious aspect just as demonstrably. We saw the Roman state take an active interest in bringing to a conclusion the theological disputes in the Christian church. The council of Nicaea called by Emperor Constantine (r. 306-337 CE) in 325 CE discussed and rejected Arius's contention that 'God the son was the first creation of God the father and thus different in being or substance…'[24] The council declared that God the father and son were 'identical in being or substance'.[25] Since Christianity was now the imperial religion, the emperor and his officials were required to enforce 'one form of Christian belief against another' following the decision at Nicaea—it was the dogma that every true Christian was now meant to adhere to. Vast resources, we are told, were expended on the exercise and those who would not come around to the formulation of Christian belief endorsed by the emperor were 'excluded from the state and its protections'.[26] Later, in 532 CE, Justinian (r. 527-565 CE), ruler of what was now the Byzantine, or the Eastern Roman Empire, began the construction of the grand basilica Hagia Sophia at Constantinople in a truly monumental display of his domain's Christian character.

Why did Augustus restore and build the shrines of deities,

---

24 Michael Kulikowski, *The Triumph of Rome. The Roman World from Hadrian to Constantine* (Cambridge, Massachusetts: Harvard University Press, 2016), p.269.

25 Ibid.

26 Ibid., p.270.

while Constantine put the whole weight of the Empire behind Christianity? With Constantine, personal piety was definitely a factor as he was a fervent Christian. But that aside, both he and his predecessor were probably using religion to achieve greater cohesion and the smooth functioning of the Roman imperium. The public ceremonials of paganism had a distinctly civic aspect to them; they sought to inspire and augment the Roman public's loyalty to the state. Standardised and officially sanctioned Christianity, on the other hand, could sure be of help in holding an enormous and diverse empire together. Religion could indeed help a state cohere and achieve greater efficacy. We witness this, for example, in England in a later, less civilized age, when the glory of Rome had passed into history. In the words of G.M. Trevelyan, one of the most celebrated historians of England, 'The early adhesion of all the English Kingdoms to the Roman system of religion [Catholicism] gave a great impetus towards racial unity, kingly and feudal power, systematic administration, legislation and taxation, and territorial as against tribal politics'.[27] In simple language, Trevelyan thinks that by backing Roman Catholicism, the English kingdoms encouraged the English racial identity and ruled more efficaciously.

Post reformation, the English state and national identity acquired further cohesion. A crucial role in this seems to have been played by the large-scale dissemination of scriptural

27 G.M. Trevelyan, *A Shortened History of England* (Penguin Books), p.64.

knowledge that was backed by the throne. At the start of the seventeenth century, the English ruler James I (r. 1603-1627) commissioned a version of the Bible (published in 1611). It largely followed an earlier text by William Tyndale which had been composed in a 'plain style' using "everyday words and proverbs," since he had wanted to be understood by the simple folk, even the 'boy that driveth the plough'.[28] Along with the Prayer Book, King James' Bible became a text that 'everyone was said to have heard, read, and memorised' in England. This made a 'standard form of English…familiar across the country, without replacing spoken dialects'.[29] 'The effect of this,' writes Robert Tombs, 'must have been powerful as a constant reminder of belonging to what has been called the "imagined community" of nationhood'.[30] All the more since, he points out, 'a sense of national identity' already existed in England.[31] A state-sponsored artefact of English Protestantism, namely King James' Bible, thus, sharpened the sense of English national identity. One assumes that this is likely to have redounded to the strength and stability of the English state.

Rulers in central and Eastern Europe similarly used religion to buttress their rule, or for its rallying value. For example, the German Emperors Henry II (r. 1014-1024) and Henry III (r. 1046-1056) 'willingly used their royal authority for the benefit

28 Robert Tombs, *The English and their History* (Penguin Books, 2014), p.197.
29 Ibid.
30 Ibid., p.200.
31 Ibid.

of the Church...'[32] They, thus, discharged the role of the 'just king' who promotes Christian culture. In return, the clergy accepted them as 'divinely appointed' rulers of the Church and leaders who would establish a Christian society.[33] The Tsars in neighbouring Russia would sometimes make an exaggerated display of their Orthodox piety. Ivan IV (r. 1547-1584), better known as 'Ivan the Terrible,' extirpated Tatar power by defeating the remaining Khanates and capturing the Tatar city of Kazan in 1552. To commemorate these achievements, he ordered the construction of the Red Square Cathedral of the Intercession. Diarmaid MacCulloch, the historian of Christianity, calls this building 'an extrovert symbol of the Tsar's joy in victory and his gratitude to Mary...the Trinity and the various saints whose intercession he had successfully invoked against the Tatars'.[34] Christianity, it seems, had served as the 'rallying rhetoric' for Ivan IV since he had evoked its pantheon of supernatural agencies and their help during a crucial phase in his reign—when he needed to muster forces against the Tatar foe. Thus, besides being a crucial prop to its strength, religion could supply the necessary rhetoric to the state when required.

Coming to India, one of the ways in which state and culture interacted here was through the king's role as the sustainer of *dharma*. As a concept, *dharma* is remarkably

32 G. Barraclough, *The Origins of Modern Germany* (New York, London: W.W. Norton & Company, 1984), p.101.

33 Ibid.

34 *Christianity. The First Three Thousand Years* (Penguin Books, 2009), p.530.

supple. However, let us give it the working definition of a cultural matrix that comprised social, moral, and political norms along with a spiritual outlook. The social norms that emanated from *dharma* pertained to the four *varnas*. One could term the *varna* order a semiotic complex, since each of the four *varnas* symbolised or 'meant' an archetypical social or economic function. The ancient Indian state, in its cultural role, was meant to be a sustainer of this semiotic complex. Thus, an epithet of the king in Sanskrit is *dharmapravartaka*, that is, one who upholds the varna-based social order.[35] The king did not just protect his subjects, *prajā*, from external danger but also maintained the 'internal structure' (of society) by upholding *varnārṣramadharma*.[36] If required, the king was meant to deploy *daṇḍa*, or coercive power wielded in the form of the army,[37] to discharge this role and extend the limits of the state. For example, *daṇḍa* was used to establish 'the ordering of society in which caste as a theory of stratification became one of the mechanisms by which the state was made acceptable in areas where no state had existed earlier…'[38] Along with the 'Brahmanical,' the king as a preserver of *dharma* was an ideal in the Buddhist tradition as well. We see Buddhist

---

35 Ram Sharan Sharma, *Aspects of Political Ideas and Institutions in Ancient India* (Delhi: Motilal Banarasidas Publishers Private Limited, 1999), 'Introduction,' p.xxvii.

36 Romila Thapar, *From Lineage to State. Social Formations in the Mid-First Millennium B.C. in the Ganga Valley* (New Delhi: OUP, 2000 [Sixth Impression]), p.129.

37 *Aspects of Political Ideas and Institutions in Ancient India*, p.36.

38 *From Lineage to State*, pp.126-127.

texts using sobriquets such as *dharmadhvaja, dharmaketu,* and *dharmādhipati* to denote the ruler.[39]

Rulers too, for their part, stressed their role as the preserver of *dharma* in its social aspect. Epigraphic evidence dating to the early centuries of the Christian era establishes that *'Dharmarāja'* was used as a proper name by several kings. Subsequently, royal epithets 'stressing the defence of the varna order' appear in inscriptions in the second century and then become common.[40] As a matter of fact, ancient Indian political thought located the origin and necessity of the state, or a designated ruling class with coercive power, in the preservation of a society organised into *varnas* with their apportioned social roles. According to about 'half a dozen Puranas,' writes R.S. Sharma, 'Brahma prescribed coercion (*daṇḍa)*...as the profession of the Kshatriyas,' so that the *varnas* performed their respective duties.[41]

Besides the *varna* order, preserving and patronising *dharma* in the form of a spiritual outlook and its semiotic expressions (commonly termed 'religion') was an important source of legitimacy for the ancient Indian polity. We see the *Arthaśāstra* of Kautilya prescribing how religious considerations ought to guide royal behaviour in various situations. The text directs the king to respect the religious sentiments and practices of the conquered peoples. He was also meant to grant their

39 *Aspects of Political Ideas and Institutions in Ancient India*, p.60.
40 Ibid., p.191.
41 Ibid., p.233.

priests several immunities as per the 'tenets' of Brahmanical society.[42] The *Arthaśāstra* also provides for the state patronage of several deities and their worship, especially enjoining the king to reserve the north of the city for its titular deity (*nagaradevatā*).[43] Another suggestion that the *Arthaśāstra* makes is for the principal gates of the capital to be named after deities such as Brahma, Indra, Yama, etc. and for places of worship and pilgrimages to be constructed within its limits.[44] In later, post-Mauryan India, we find the Kushanas making an 'unambiguous declaration of the religion they professed'.[45] For example, the Kushana ruler Kadphises I termed himself *dharmāthidāsa*, probably on account of his devotion to the *dharma* of the Buddha. Bhagawan Shiva too was represented on the Kushana coins.[46] Ancient Indian states and their rulers, thus, projected a cultural intent through visible identification with a range of evocative, conspicuous, and potent symbols (which the *varna* order, sacred architecture, pilgrimages, and deities were).

Moving on, the cultural persona of the ancient Indian state had a linguistic aspect to it in the form of Sanskrit. Sheldon Pollock writes that the Sanskrit language formed a 'way of speaking about and conceiving of the nature of political

42 Ibid., p.255.
43 Ibid., p.256.
44 Ibid.
45 Ibid., p.308.
46 Ibid.

power'[47] in an enormous cosmopolis that encompassed the whole of the Indian Subcontinent and Southeast Asia. This development occurred as there emerged by the fifth century CE 'a linguistically homogenous and conceptually standardised form of Sanskrit political poetry'.[48] This 'political poetry' was of two kinds—*kāvya* and *praśasti*. 'Published' as inscriptions and used to announce the glorious deeds, victories, valour, and virtues of rulers through these verse forms, Sanskrit became a standard way of communicating political will and a means to the 'aestheticization of power'[49] in the cosmopolis in which it obtained. One reason behind this, according to Pollock, was Sanskrit's remarkable communicative capacity. Due to the 'formal and rhetorical attributes' that it possessed, Sanskrit could make a reality, in a way, more real by rendering it 'more noticeable, more complex, more beautiful…'[50] Sanskrit, in other words, was very good at enriching reality, very likely because of its capacity to generate meanings out of it. Consequent to this, Sanskrit was considered a 'very appropriate vehicle for the expression of royal will' and it came to be expected of kings to acquire felicity in the language.[51] In other words, Sanskrit in ancient India was a remarkably evocative symbol of cultural power, and royal authority was meant to know how to wield it. We do indeed find rulers in ancient Indian history who used

---

47 Sheldon Pollock, *The Language of the Gods in the World of Men. Sanskrit, Culture and Power in Premodern India* (Ranikhet: Permanent Black, 2007 [Third Impression]), p.115.

48 Ibid., p.122.

49 Ibid., p.132.

50 Ibid., p.255.

51 Ibid.

the Sanskrit language with great dexterity. For instance, some of the Gupta kings were 'Sanskrit poets of no mean order,' that is, they were quite competent at composing verses in Sanskrit.[52]

It is probable that, besides being connoisseurs and practitioners of Sanskrit literature, the Gupta kings also sought to invest their persons with a certain divinity. This is evidenced in the *Raghuvaṃśam*, allegedly a Gupta era text, that identifies the ruler with the deities.[53] Moving down a few centuries, we see that identification with cultural symbols such as shrines and deities was often vital to the formation and functioning of states in early medieval India. This was indeed so in South India in a big way. For example, James Heitzman writes about the Chola state, that it displayed characteristics of the 'ritual segmentary state'. That is, the Chola kings sought to unite 'disparate' and 'autonomous' local leaders 'under a single, mediating agency through ritual means'. These involved granting royal protection to religious institutions (by making them tax-free grants and constructing shrines) and arbitrating local disputes 'typically involving' religious institutions.[54] The Cholas, thus, represented 'a style of dharmic kingship'.[55]

---

52 V.V. Mirashi, 'Some Royal Poets of the Vākātaka Age,' in Kunal Chakrabarti and Kanad Sinha, eds., *State, Power & Legitimacy* (Delhi: Primus Books, 2019), p.802

53 See Kumkum Roy, 'Seeing and Hearing. Representations of Kingship in the *Abhijñāśakuntalam* and the *Raghuvaṃśam* of Kalidasa'. Ibid, p.763.

54 'State Formation in South India. 850-1280' in Hermann Kulke, ed., *The State in India. 1000-1700* (New Delhi: OUP, 2004 [Third Impression]), p.191. Heitzman built on a model originally developed by Berton Stein.

55 Burton Stein, *Peasant State and Society in Medieval South India* (Delhi: OUP, 1980), p.45.

The king, as it seems, could project authority upon disparate local chiefs and unite the realm by intervening in the administration of religious institutions, or temples. In this sense, temples were enablers of kingly power in early medieval India. Alongside, temples came to play other, very important roles in the early medieval polities. Being 'a symbol in material space of the sacred domain,' the temple could be an instrument for the king to (temporally?) approximate that domain by identifying with the deity enshrined in it. This practice was begun by the Pallavas and 'augmented' by the Cholas. Or, the king could rule as the 'agent' of the deity placed in the temple, apparently in search of greater authority and legitimacy. The Gajapati king Anangabhima III (r. 1211-1238 CE), for example, did the same by surrendering his temporal powers to Bhagawan Jagannatha.[56] When a ruler sought to establish an imperial realm, he again did so by putting himself in vassalage to a deity. For instance, as an 'imperial lord,' or *mahārājadhiraja*, he would style himself the earthly representative 'of the tutelary deity (*raṣtradevatā*) of the kingdom,' usually Bhagawan Shiva or Vishnu. The tutelary deity was fitted out with the symbols of an 'earthly maharaja' and the temple rites were assimilated into the palace rites.[57] It has been argued that the construction of several large, monumental temples such as Rajarajeshvara

56 Brajadulal Chattopadhyaya, 'Political Processes and the Structure of Polity in Early Medieval India'. *The State in India. 1000-1700*, p.210.

57 Hermann Kulke, 'The Early and the Imperial Kingdom: A Processural Model of Integrative State Formation in Early Medieval India'. Ibid, p.258.

and Lingaraja as regional kingdoms attained the height of their power (between 1000 and 1250 CE) testifies to the process of titular deities being assigned a political role.[58]

The political or temporal role of the 'titular deity' of a state was taken very seriously indeed. In 1354, Bukka, one of the founders of the Vijayanagara kingdom, made Virupaksha, a form of Bhagawan Shiva, the state deity. So devoted were Vijayanagara rulers to Virupaksha that important state documents bore his 'signature'.[59] Richard Eaton suggests that the Vijayanagara state was imagined as a unique sacred space on account of its association with Virupaksha.[60] Along with the shrine of Virupaksha, the Vijayanagara kings supported the Ramchandra temple, which probably served as the 'state chapel' and the focal point of a 'spatially articulated political theology' and identified the ruler with Shri Rama.[61] Again, the annual Vijayadashami festival was very important for the Vijayanagara kings. On this occasion, they honoured 'worthy Brahmans, the astrologer, and the purohita,' and held sports of elephants, horses, and foot soldiers.[62] Through this grand display, the Vijayanagara kings incorporated 'the disparate

58 Ibid.

59 Rchard Eaton, *India in the Persianate Age* (Allen Lane, an Imprint of Penguin Books, 2019), p.87.

60 'The Articulation of Islamic Space in Medieval Deccan' in *Essays on Islam and Indian History* (New Delhi: OUP, 2000), pp.159-175.

61 Sheldon Pollock, 'Ramayana and the Political Imagination in India' in *The Journal of Asian* Studies, Vol. 52, No. 2 (May, 1993), p.268

62 Nicholas B. Dirks, *The Hollow Crown. Ethnohistory of an Indian Kingdom* (Cambridge, New York, New Rochelle, Melbourne, Sydney: CUP, 2008), p.40.

elements of the kingdom into [their] sovereign being... rendering them all parts—metonyms—of [themselves]...'[63] The power of the Vijayanagara sovereign was thus culturally amplified and communicated across the realm through some spectacular symbolic displays.

Based on what we observe in the European and Indian situations, we suggest that states may be termed 'culture-power formations'. As we see, the modern linguistic nation-state primarily wields language, while the premodern state mainly utilised religion, to fulfil the expediencies of rule, or power enforcement. States, thus, represent specific alliances of culture and power. Culture buttresses and provides pathways to state power. Or, one might say that culture, in the hands of the state, is the 'capillary force' of the power embodied by it. State power, on the other hand, undergirds culture. This symbiosis of state and culture, as we see, is because both seek to regulate and order human behaviour. They both, to borrow some Foucauldian phrases, are modes of action upon human actions, or forms of conduct upon conducts.[64] State and culture, in this sense, one might say, share a certain 'essence'.

UNDERSTANDING THE 'ISLAMICATE'

Let us make it clear that we are not using the term narrowly to merely denote Muslim religious beliefs, practices, and theology (though the 'Islamicate' will surely include these). The term was

63 Ibid., p.42.

64 *Power. Essential Works. 1954-84*, pp.340-341.

originally coined by Marshall Hodgson, the author of a grand, three volume history of Islam. He understood the Islamicate as 'a *culture*, centred on a lettered tradition, which has been historically distinctive of Islamdom the *society*, and which has been naturally shared in by both Muslims and non-Muslims who participate at all fully in the society of Islamdom'.[65] Simply put, Hodgson primarily saw the Islamicate as a literary, or literate, tradition, historically characteristic of Muslim society, but which could potentially include non-Muslims in its fold. Like us, he did not take a narrowly religious view of the Islamicate. The term would, he explained, 'refer not directly to the religion, Islam, itself, but to the social and cultural complex historically associated with Islam and the Muslims, both among Muslims themselves and even when found among non-Muslims'.[66] As a social and cultural complex, the Islamicate could express itself through a language such as Urdu. Being the purveyor of a rich 'lettered tradition,' it has always involved very fair numbers of non-Muslims. After all, one of the most well-known Urdu litterateurs is Munshi Premchand, a Hindu. 'If one could not refer to it [Urdu] as Islamicate,' writes Hodgson, 'one could say it was a language of the culture of Islamdom'.[67] Now, this is crucial, since, as it seems to us, Hodgson means that the Islamicate is the same as

---

65 Marshal G. S. Hodgson, *The Venture of Islam. Conscience and History in a World Civilization. Vol. 1, The Classical Age of Islam* (Chicago and London: The University of Chicago Press, 1977), p.58. Italics in original.

66 Ibid., p.59.

67 Ibid.

'the culture of Islamdom'. In that case, along with Urdu, it is possible to identify so many other instances, or components, of the Islamicate—the Persian language and literary forms, Islamic architecture, the courtly practices and ceremonials of Muslim-ruled states, the conceptions of sovereignty and legitimate kingship sought to be developed with reference to Islam, Islamic jurisprudence, theology, and devotions, Muslim attitudes towards non-Muslims and their religious beliefs, and a rather heterodox mode of spirituality such as Sufism, just to name a few.

The 'Islamicate,' it seems, may be understood as so many artefacts, traditions, practices, ideas, and forms of behaviour broadly associable with Muslims, all of them deployable as powerful and evocative symbols. The Islamicate, thus, is a cultural matrix rooted in the social body of Islam.

The Islamicate cultural matrix might find some participation, room, or accommodation, for non-Muslims, but only, it seems, as subordinate or marginal partners (as a historical survey might suggest). For example, Islamic jurisprudence and conceptions of sovereignty could accommodate non-Muslims only as *zimmis*; Muslim attitudes towards non-Muslim religiosity have been mostly ambivalent (even hostile), and Islamicate literary cultures (be it Persian or Urdu) only touched the elite fringe of non-Muslim societies (among Hindus they involved mostly Kayasths, Khatris, and Kashmiri Pandits).

THE SYMBOLIC WAYS OF THE 'ISLAMICATE' STATE FORM

An Arab army led by Muhammad bin Qasim marched into and conquered upper Sind early in 712 CE. A nearly three-century-long interlude followed before India had a second significant encounter with Muslim arms. This was in 1000 CE, when Mahmud of Ghazni, ruler of a small principality in Afghanistan, commenced the first of his (what eventually became) yearly military forays into India. It was during one of them that, in 1025 CE, he ventured all the way to Somnath on Gujarat's southern coast and sacked and destroyed the famous Shiva temple there. Till he died in 1030 CE, he repeatedly raided and pillaged North India and incorporated Punjab and parts of Sind into his dominion.[68]

Ghaznavid rule in India turned out to be relatively short-lived though. It ended in 1186 when Muhammad Ghuri took Lahore from the Ghaznavids. In 1192 he defeated Prithviraj Chauhan in the battle of Tarain (after being bested by him the previous year at the same place). Later, his slave Qutb al-Din Aibek conquered Delhi, the Chauhan capital. This laid the foundations of the 'Delhi sultanate'. Aibek became its ruler (r. 1206-10) after his master was assassinated in 1206[69] and inaugurated what is called the Mamluk or 'slave' dynasty (followed by the Khalji, Tughlaq, Sayyid, and Lodhi dynasties). This was the historical moment when, we will say,

68 S.A.A. Rizvi, *The Wonder that was India II* (Picador India, 2018), p.15.

69 Richard M. Eaton, *India in the Persianate Age. 1000-1765* (Allen Lane, 2019), pp. 40-44.

the Islamicate state form, a distinct culture-power formation, was truly planted in India. The new state transformed Delhi's sacred spaces as Aibek constructed the Quwwat-ul-Islam Mosque at Mihirapuri (alternatively Mihirapalli, currently known as Mehrauli) using the masonry of twenty-seven 'pre-existing Hindu and Jain temples'.[70] Unlike the ancient and early medieval Indian state, the Delhi sultanate was not a patron and preserver of the shrines of deities (though we learn that Aibek's master, Muhammad Ghuri, had issued coins bearing the image of Devi Lakshmi).[71] As a matter of fact, it appears to be a pattern that the annexation of new territory to the Delhi Sultanate was followed by the destruction of temples. When Qutb al-Din Mubarak Khalaji (r. 1316-20) defeated the Yadava dynasty in 1318, he constructed a 'grand congregational mosque' in their capital Devagiri 'stripping' one-hundred-and-seventy-seven columns from 'Hindu and Jain temples nearby'.[72] According to Richard Eaton, the 'grand' mosque at Devagiri 'projected Delhi's political presence in this distant province...'[73] Not long after Qutb al-Din, Prince Ulugh Khan, son of Sultan Giyath al-Din Tughlaq (r. 1320-25), sought to project Delhi's 'political presence' into another distant territory the same way. He captured Warangal, the Kakatiya capital, in the Telugu heartland and destroyed the great temple of

70 Meenakshi Jain, *Flight of Deities and Rebirth of Temples* (New Delhi: Aryan Books International, 2019), p.56.

71 *India in the Persianate Age*, p.43.

72 Ibid., p.65.

73 Ibid.

Svayambhu Shiva that it was known for. He dismantled this structure 'to its foundations' and used its masonry to construct a 'large congregational mosque'.[74] The Delhi Sultanate, we deduce, restricted the public cultural displays of its non-Muslim subjects by violating their 'sacred spaces,' or shrines. Further, it continued to broadcast its authority through monumental mosques. We identify these as instances of semiotics, or culture, that the Islamicate state form deployed in the Indian context to project an image of a 'triumphant Islam'.

A little digression before we move on, Richard Eaton claims that attacking a temple patronised by an enemy king had been 'integrated into Indian political behaviour' since the sixth century CE.[75] Seemingly, he is urging that we ought to see the foregoing instances of temple destruction as the continuation of an age-old practice resorted to by Hindu rulers. But should we? Meenakshi Jain compellingly argues that we should not. What Hindu rulers carried out, she writes, when they attacked a temple in an enemy kingdom, was 'image appropriation'.[76] That is, they carried away the *vigraha* and installed it in a grand temple of their own. For example, she points out, Yashovarman, the Chandella ruler (r. 925-50 CE) seized an image of Vaikuntha Vishnu from the Pratihara ruler, Devapala, and installed it in the Lakshmana (Vaikuntha)

74 Ibid., pp.67-68.

75 *Temple Desecration and Muslim States in Medieval India* (New Delhi: Hope India, 2004), p.32.

76 *Flight of Deities and Rebirth of Temples*, p.18.

temple at Khajuraho,[77] while several Chalukya and Kalinga icons were placed in the Gangaikondacholapuram temple complex built by Rajendra Chola I[78] (r. 1014-1044; these icons were likely to have been acquired during military campaigns). Muslim rulers, on the other hand, were said to have destroyed 'entire temples, and where that was not possible, disfigured the images'.[79] Further, we have seen above that, not just Hindu, but Jain temples, which were unlikely to have been built and patronized by a dynasty, too were destroyed (in Delhi and Devagiri). Hence, we are inclined to think that the iconoclasm practised by the Delhi Sultanate uniquely belonged to an 'Islamicate' cultural discourse of power.[80]

---

77 Ibid., p.11.

78 Ibid., p.12.

79 Ibid., p.18.

80 Richard Eaton provides just one instance of a destruction of a temple by a Hindu ruler, that of the Rashrakuta king Indra III (r. 914-29 CE) demolishing the Kalapriya temple built by the rival Pratihara dynasty. In every other example of 'temple desecration' committed by a Hindu ruler that he cites we see that a *vigraha* ('idol') was merely 'seized' from one temple and moved to another (*Temple Desecration and Muslim States in Medieval India*, pp.36-37). This makes us feel that Meenakshi Jain is spot on with her contention. Jain herself manages to discover just two Hindu rulers who assailed temples, both belonging to Kashmir—Sankara Varman (r. 883-902 CE) of the Utpala dynasty and Harsa (r. 1089-1111) of the Lohara dynasty. Sankara Varman, however, restricted himself to appropriating 'temple lands and treasures,' meaning that he committed neither desecration or demolitions of shrines, while Harsa appears to have been influenced by 'Turuskas,' or Muslims (*Flight of Deities and Rebirth of Temples*, pp.16-17). Quite obviously, it appears to us, Hindu rulers desecrated, leave alone demolished, temples very rarely indeed (if ever). Just three examples dredged from many thousand years long history of Hindu kingship are just not sufficient to persuade us to believe otherwise.

Moving on, an individual ruler of the Delhi Sultanate could place his actions within a paradigm of Islamicate symbolism, or cultural ideals, apparently to lend his authority greater salience and validity. Shams al-Din Iltutmish (r. 1211-1236), for example, 'instituted a full-fledged department, with *qazis, muftis*, and *sheikh al-Islam*, to deal with religious matters. He built mosques and *madrasas* to strengthen the foundations of his rule'.[81] 'Iltutmish was close to the *ulāma* too,' writes Sunil Kumar, 'since he shared their concern regarding the imposition of the *Shari'ā* in his domains'.[82] He used the *Shari'ā* as a justification for charging *jizyāh* and also destroyed some old temples on the ground that they were 'beguiling' Muslims.[83] Apparently, he sought to pose as a Sultan who performs the 'dual role of conqueror and protector of the holy law (*shari'a*)'.[84] Reportedly, he also rued the fact that 'Muslims, in terms of strength, were still like salt in a dish and thus unable to wage an all-out war either to force infidels to accept Islam or to exterminate them because of their refusal'.[85] The cultural persona of the state he ruled made such posturing necessary. 'Since Islam,' writes S.

81 Muzaffar Alam, *The Languages of Political Islam in India* (Delhi: Ashoka University in association with Permanent Black, 2016 [Fourth Paperback Impression]), p.84.

82 *The Emergence of the Delhi Sultanate* (Permanent Black in association with Ashoka University, 2007), p.226

83 Satish Chandra, 'Society, Culture, and the State in Medieval India: An Essay in Interpretation' in *Essays on Medieval Indian History* (New Delhi: OUP, 2005), p.46.

84 *The Emergence of the Delhi Sultanate*, p.226.

85 *The Languages of Political Islam in India*, p.42.

Nurul Hasan, 'provided a powerful binding force for the ruling classes,' the Sultan had to 'take some demonstrative steps to show to his co-religionists that he was ruling in accordance with the laws of Islam'.[86] He does not seem to have had much of a choice in this regard as, according to Raziuddin Aquil, there was a 'general perception among Muslims in the Delhi Sultanate that it was 'their' government...'[87]

Sometimes, the textual discourse of power (in the Foucauldian sense of being a 'totality of effective statements')[88] prevailing in the Delhi sultanate appears to have been developed with reference to a cultural imagination of what a 'correct' Muslim ruler ought to do. For example, Ziya al-Din Barani (1285-1358), author of *Fatawā-I Jahāndārī* and courtier and companion of Muhammad bin Tughlaq (r. 1324-51) declared that a 'good Muslim king should not be content with merely levying the *jizyah* and *kharaj* on Hindus'. Barani preferred that he should instead go to the extent of establishing 'the supreme position of Islam by overthrowing infidelity [Hinduism] and slaughtering its leaders (*imams*), the Brahmans'.[89] Barani seems to have been quite a pious man and Muzaffar Alam, one of the most well-known historians of medieval India, writes that in

86 'Aspects of State and Religion in Medieval India' in Satish Chandra, ed., *Religion, State, and Society in Medieval India. Collected Works of S. Nurul Hasan* (New Delhi: OUP, 2005), p.65.

87 Raziuddin Aquil, *Sufism, Culture and Politics. Afghans and Islam in Medieval North India* (New Delhi: OUP, 2020 [Sixteenth Impression]), p.11.

88 Michel Foucault, *The Archeology of Knowledge* (Routledge, 2009), p.29.

89 *The Languages of Political Islam in India*, p.37.

his world there could only be two life patterns diametrically opposed to each other, one in conformity with the *shari'ā* and the other against it. 'Barani slotted,' Alam further writes, 'even the normal, universal, human qualities into binary oppositions—Islamic and anti-Islamic, or *shar'i* and *ghair-shar'i*'.[90] As far as Barani was concerned, *zawābit*, or secular state regulations, were valid only as far as they were expedient measures undertaken in situations in which 'Muslim rulers were unable to implement the regulations of the *Shari'ā* in full'.[91] His acute concern for the *Shari'ā* actually made his attitude towards temporal authority somewhat ambivalent. Barani thought that the institution of the sultanate had no place in *Shari'ā* and that it restricted its operation. However, he still regarded the sultanate necessary for the survival of the *Shari'ā*.[92]

While it intervened in and violated the 'sacred spaces' of the non-Muslims, the Delhi Sultanate closely associated itself with the spiritual charisma of Muslim holy men, or the Sufis. Eaton informs us that 'in every provincial centre of the sultanate there resided a Sufi sheikh who belonged to one or another spiritual order [of Sufis]…'[93] They were not lone rangers distributing spiritual merit but 'very much connected to metropolitan Delhi'.[94] It seems like a network of Sufis fanned

90 Ibid.

91 Ibid., p.40.

92 M. Athar Ali, *Mughal India. Studies in Polity, Ideas, Society and Culture* (New Delhi: OUP, 2008), p.123.

93 *India in the Persianate Age*, p.74.

94 Ibid., pp.74-75.

out from Delhi nearly replicating the administrative network of the Delhi Sultanate, and the two overlapped. Eaton writes that prominent Sufis of Delhi sent out their leading disciples to the provincial centres who were then patronised by the governors posted there.[95] The Sultans sought proximity to the Sufis too. Ghiyas-ud-Din-Balban (r. 1266-87), for example, was a devotee of Farid-ud-Din Ganj-i-Shakar.[96] The Lodi Sultans dined in the company of the Sufis.[97] The Sufis, on the other hand, often subserved the Sultans' interests. They would participate in military campaigns and even give suggestions as to how they might be prosecuted successfully.[98]

Persian flourished in the Delhi Sultanate. Aziz Ahmad tells us that Delhi became the principal centre of Persian poetry in the thirteenth century (and retained this position till the eighteenth). Persian language versifiers such as Taj-ad-din Sangriza and Shihab-ad-din Mahmara found patronage at the court of Iltutmish.[99] Amir Khusrau, the most famous Indian poet in the Persian language, too lived in Delhi as a disciple of the Sufi sheikh Nizam al-Din Auliya.[100] Persian language historiography too found a favourable atmosphere in the Delhi Sultanate. To give a few examples of the most famous historians and the histories that one associates with them,

95 Ibid. p.75.
96 *Sufism, Culture and Politics*, p.122.
97 Ibid., pp.174-175.
98 Ibid., p.175.
99 *An Intellectual History of Islam in India* (Edinburgh University Press, 1969), p.73.
100 *India in the Persianate Age*, p.75.

there is Minhaj-al-Siraj al-Juzjani and his *Tabaqat-I Nasiri*, a work dealing with the Ghurids and early Mamluk Sultans in particular,[101] Hasan Nizami's *Tājal-ma'āthir*, which deals with the reign of Aibek, and Barani's *Tā'rikh-I Firuz Shāhi* which concerns itself 'exclusively with Indo-Muslim history'.[102] The rulers of the Delhi Sultanate, much like the Ghaznavids, appear to have been 'Persophiles' (to coin a word on the lines of 'Anglophile' and 'Francophile'). Persian was the language of cultural power *par excellence* in this age, just as Sanskrit was in ancient India.

We seem to be now in a position to identify certain standard semiotic resources, or cultural aspects, of the Islamicate state form, or culture-power formation, as it came to be in North India. These could be projecting sovereignty through monumental Islamic architecture and curtailment of the public cultural displays or 'sacred spaces,' of non-Muslims using a discourse or imagery that harkened to 'Islam' as a preferred cultural ideal to amplify, legitimate, and moralise royal authority, a preference for the Persian language ('Persophilia'), and association with the spiritual potency of Sufis.[103] The Delhi Sultanate routed its

101 *An Intellectual History of Islam in India*, p.69.

102 Ibid., p.80.

103 The regional Sultanates that emerged in India in the fourteenth century displayed an 'Islamicate' cultural aspect too. For example, the Bahmani and Bengal sultanates were closely associated with Sufi shaikhs of the Chisti order (Temple Desecration and Muslim States, p.26). Then, the regional sultanates showed a preference for Persian. Sultan Zain al-'Abidin (r. 1418-70) made Persian the official state language of Kashmir, while it was the language of civil administration in the Sultanate of Malwa (India in the Persianate Age, pp.118 & 125).

power through the foregoing symbolic tropes, and projected a cultural persona, just as states in Europe and India historically acquired efficacious power and a cultural persona through a Christian moral and visual rhetoric, association with the *varna* order, shrines, deities, and the Sanskrit language.

We think that the Islamicate character of the Delhi Sultanate was a constant, in the sense that it adopted the symbolic forms and practices identified above to project a particular cultural persona, even if it had individual rulers who did not seem to have been very orthodox Muslims. For example, Sultan Balban of the Mamluk dynasty (r. 1266-87) declared that, since he could neither act as a defender of the faith (*dinpanāh*) nor follow the religious commandments (*dindāri*), it was enough for him to dispense justice (*adl*),[104] while Muhammad bin Tughlaq (r. 1325-51) chatted with yogis and played Holi.[105] Besides being ruled by Sultans who were not very observant Muslims, the Delhi Sultanate sometimes made major cultural concessions to the non-Muslims as well. But testifying to its unvarying 'Islamicate' cultural persona, the authors of these concessions legitimated them within specifically Muslim notions of fairness and justice. For instance, when the 'well-established religious practices' of the Hindus were guaranteed by the *ulāmā* of the Delhi Sultanate (in the reign of Sikandar Lodi, 1489-1517) we note that it was done with reference to the *shari'ā*.[106]

104 *Religion, State, and Society in Medieval India*, p.67.

105 M. Athar Ali, *Mughal India*, p.34.

106 Satish Chandra, 'Society, Culture, and the State in Medieval India: An Essay in Interpretation' in *Essays on Medieval Indian History*, p.47.

THE MUGHAL EMPIRE AS AN 'ISLAMICATE' STATE FORM

Babur (r. 1526-1530), the founder of the Mughal Empire, was not queasy about making a belligerent show of his piety. We learn from Satish Chandra, one of the most important historians of medieval India, that he declared the battle against Rana Sanga (fought at Khanwa, Rajasthan, in 1527) to be a '*jihād*'. Following the battle, he also raised a heap of the skulls of the enemy soldiers his army had slaughtered.[107] Maybe, he was making a grand display of the number of unbelievers he had dispatched. No doubt, like its predecessor, the Delhi Sultanate, the Mughal Empire turned out to be an 'Islamicate' state form in every sense. This is noticeable, to begin with, in the way a Mughal ruler morally constructed and validated his authority. For example, historians Shashi Joshi and Bhagwan Josh say that the 'dominant discourse' legitimising a Mughal ruler's 'political and economic position' was one of Islam.[108] This is true for the Mughal Empire even under Akbar (r. 1556-1605), apparently the most culturally broad-minded and tolerant of Mughal rulers. Though a mature Akbar seemingly tried to make the non-Muslims genuine stakeholders in the Empire by promoting the ideal of *sulh-i-kul* (amity among faiths), we shall argue that the Mughal Empire still very much remained an Islamicate enterprise in his hands. According to Joshi and Josh,

107 *Medieval India. From the Sultanat to the Mughals. Part Two* (1526-1748) (New Delhi: Har-Anand Publications, 2000), p.44.

108 *Struggle for Hegemony in India, Vol. 3, Culture Community and Power* (New Delhi: Sage Publications, 1994), p.72.

Akbar sought to 'go beyond the attempt to secure passive loyalty and reconciliation; to achieve a new sense of accommodation, symbiosis and participatory loyalty by addressing the balance of power between communities'. Yet, they write, 'the cultural environment of the Mughal Empire remained suffused with Islam'.[109] The Cambridge historian C.A. Bayly echoes his Indian counterparts when he speculates that 'what Akbar was perhaps trying to do was build a specifically Indian imperial patriotism in the context of the broader sovereignty of Islam'.[110] In popular consciousness, Akbar was the perfect foil for Aurangzeb, but both rulers, Joshi and Josh argue, enforced the hegemony of Islam. They employed different means, however. The 'basis of Akbar's cultural expansiveness,' write the two historians, 'was a conception of hegemony resting on an equilibrium of cultural norms which acknowledged the cultural stamp of Islam on the Mughal state's political hegemony without threatening the cultural practices of non-Muslim peoples'.[111] In other words, they say, the Mughal Empire projected a 'soft' hegemony of Islam under Akbar. This is because we see that Akbar's approach was rather accommodative and gave cultural room to the non-Muslims. Aurangzeb, on the other hand, transformed the character of the Mughal imperium and brought it under a 'hard' hegemony of Islam. Joshi and Josh contend that Aurangzeb's

109 Ibid., p.171.

110 *Origins of Nationality in South Asia: Patriotism and Ethical Government in the Making of Modern India* (New Delhi: OUP, 2001), p.38.

111 *Struggle for Hegemony in India*, Vol. 3, p.97.

'paradigm of cultural hegemony' was about implementing the 'ideological-cultural nucleus of Islamic culture' that the strong authority of *ulāmā* embodied to give sanction and legitimacy to Mughal rule.[112]

Let us now begin to delineate the 'Islamicate' persona of the Mughal state in some detail. To start with, it seems that sovereignty was framed and projected in the Mughal Empire with reference to Muslim history and convention. One notices, for example, that 'Delhi and Agra were designed respectively as *dar al-khalifa* and *mustaqarr al-khalifa*, and the Mughal emperor was not infrequently called *khalifa*'.[113] Though Muzaffar Alam assures us that Mughal historians did not quite see the Mughal emperors as caliphs of Muslims, the very fact that they could be imagined in such a manner seems to suggest that in the eyes of the believers, their persons carried resonances relevant to them. We hazard this guess because we notice that the Mughal emperors 'prided in calling themselves the Majesty and Light of the Faith (Jalal al-Din Akbar, Nur al-Din Jahangir)' and made 'periodic dispatch of rich donations to the holy cities of Mecca and Medina…'[114]

If the Mughal rulers were imagined as caliphs and their persons resonated with believers, it must have been because 'Islam' often inspired or framed their actions serving as a paradigm of culturally desirable conduct, or ideals (from a

112 Ibid., p.97.

113 *The Languages of Political Islam in India*, p.14.

114 Ibid., p.78.

peculiarly Muslim point of view). In 1568, after conquering Chittor, Akbar issued a proclamation reviling infidels. He also imposed the *jizyā* on non-Muslims in 1575.[115] Further, there is evidence in the *Akbar Nāma* and Āin-i-Akbari of the forcible conversion of Hindus to Islam during Akbar's reign.[116] In 1579, Akbar sought to 'assume the position of an interpreter of Islamic law and, in spheres where the existing corpus was silent, of a legislator' through the *mahza,*[117] which was a statement or testimony signed by the theologians recognising that Akbar had a particular religious status.[118] Nevertheless, Akbar was not puritanical in the religious sense and did have an inclination for Sufism, which probably accounted for a mystical experience he had had while on a hunt the previous year. But, writes Athar Ali, this experience 'was altogether within the Islamic framework'. This is why, when he built a pavilion and laid a garden around it to commemorate it, he called the place 'Little Mecca' (*Makkā-i Khurd*).[119] Akbar's enlightened religious outlook, or '*Sulh-i Kul,*' too seems to have evolved within an Islamicate framework as it had him employing 'the terminology of Sufi silsilahs' and calling his 'spiritual followers iradat-gazinan or murids'.[120] Very likely, he was 'aspiring to a position analogous

---

115 M. Athar Ali, 'Sulh-I Kul and the Religious Ideas of Akbar,' Mughal India, p.159.

116 Sri Ram Sharma, *The Religious Policy of the Mughal Emperors* (Humphrey Milford. OUP, 1940), p.16.

117 M. Athar Ali, 'Towards an Interpretation of the Mughal Empire,' *Mughal India*, p.63.

118 M. Athar Ali, 'Sulh-I Kul and the Religious Ideas of Akbar,' Ibid., p.159.

119 M. Athar Ali, 'The 'Vision' in the Salt Range, 1578. An Interpretation,' Ibid., p.154.

120 M. Athar Ali, 'Sulh-I Kul and the Religious Ideas of Akbar,' Ibid., p.163.

to a murshid, or spiritual guide of an elite set of disciples...'[121] In fact, S.A.A. Rizvi opines that Akbar's mind was filled with religious orthodoxy and his 'liberal measures' merely tried 'divorcing personal religious beliefs from the public good'.[122]

Moving on to Jahangir (r. 1605-1627), he carried on in much the same vein as his father. Among the achievements of his reign are listed the consolidation of the bases of the 'glorious community' and enforcement of the precepts of the 'illustrious *shari'a*'.[123] When he invaded Mewar, he termed it a religious war.[124] Through various measures, Jahangir sought to portray himself as the 'protector of the true faith'. To mention a few, he allegedly gave (according to the Jesuits) daily allowances to those converting to Islam, put an end to Hindu men marrying Muslim women at Rajauri, and pardoned certain prisoners if they turned Muslim.[125] His execution of Sikh Guru Arjun Dev is, of course, well known. Besides, he persecuted the Jains of Gujarat.[126] No doubt, Jahangir was, for all intents and purposes, to a majority of his subjects, a good Muslim.[127]

Like the Delhi Sultanate, the Mughal Empire curtailed the public cultural displays of the non-Muslims. Their shrines, or 'sacred spaces,' were thus frequently targeted for erasure. Jahangir had a temple of Varaha destroyed during a visit to

---

121 Ibid.

122 *The Wonder that was India*, p.106.

123 *The Languages of Political Islam in India*, p.77.

124 *The Wonder that was India*, p.116.

125 *The Religious Policy of the Mughal Emperors*, p.72.

126 Ibid., p.78.

127 Ibid., p.89.

Ajmer.[128] Further, temples were destroyed at Kangra, Pushkar, and Mewar during his reign.[129] Upon acceding to the throne, Shah Jahan asserted the 'fundamentally Islamic character of the [Mughal] state...'[130] He styled himself the 'Protector of Islam' and banned the construction of new temples.[131] In his Sixth Regnal Year (1633), he ordered that 'no temple whose foundation had been laid in Jahangir's time but had not been completed would be allowed to be completed'.[132] Shahjahan (r. 1627-1658) also destroyed a fair number of temples—three in Gujarat, seventy-two in Benaras and its vicinity, and four elsewhere in the province of Allahabad. A few temples were pulled down in Kashmir too.[133] His son, Aurangzeb (r. 1658-1707), continued with the policy of not allowing the construction of new temples. At the same time, he destroyed several old shrines. For example, he had the temple at Somnath demolished in 1665.[134] The destruction of old shrines became more frequent as Aurangzeb's reign grew embattled and he had to pacify uprisings by the Jats and the Marathas. He, it seems, came to consider it to be 'legitimate to destroy even long-standing Hindu temples as a measure of punishment and as a warning'.[135]

128 Ibid., p.73.

129 Ibid., p.89.

130 Satish Chandra, 'Jizyah and the State in Indian during the Seventeenth Century' in *Essays on Medieval Indian History*, pp.316-317.

131 Satish Chandra, 'State and Composite Culture in Pluralistic Society' in *State, Society, and Culture in Indian History* (New Delhi: OUP, 2012), p.35.

132 Satish Chandra, *Medieval India*, pp.254-255.

133 *The Religious Policy of the Mughal Emperors*, p.103.

134 Ibid., p.137.

135 Ibid., 278.

That is probably why he destroyed the Vishwanath and Keshav Rai temples (at Benaras and Mathura respectively) when the Jat rebellion broke out (1669). Apparently, Aurangzeb had begun to 'look upon the preservation of prominent temples as a kind of guarantee of good conduct on the part of the Hindus' of a particular area.[136] So, whatever limited rights to cultural display the non-Muslims possessed in Aurangzeb's reign, it looks like they were contingent on their political docility. Sometimes, it seems, Aurangzeb demolished temples just to make a point. After he annexed the state of Jodhpur in 1679 upon the death of Maharaja Jaswant Singh, many temples were demolished there by his emissary Khan-i-Jahan. This was, as it appears, 'an announcement that the State was no longer being governed by a Hindu raja but had now passed into imperial hands'.[137] And then, seemingly, Aurangzeb destroyed temples out of plain spite and whimsy, having once ordered the pulling down of temples in the friendly state of Jaipur. When on the way to the Deccan in 1681, he ordered the destruction of all temples en route.[138] Certain Hindu festivals were curbed too, for example, the celebration of Holi and Diwali were banned by an imperial decree in 1665.[139] In 1672-73, Aurangzeb resumed all grants held by Hindus.[140]

---

136 Satish Chandra, 'Reassessing Aurangzeb' in *State, Society, and Culture in Indian History*, p.132.

137 *The Religious Policy of the Mughal Emperors*, p.144.

138 Ibid., p.145.

139 Ibid., p.150.

140 *The Agrarian System of Mughal India* (New Delhi: OUP, 1999), p.357. Only very occasional relaxations of the decree appear to have been made, in case of the Govind Dev temple and the priest of the Madan Mohan temple.

The latter part of Aurangzeb's reign demonstrates the extent to which 'Islam' as a paradigm of culturally desirable conduct, or ideals could be expedient for a Mughal ruler (on account of the 'Islamicate' persona of the state). In fact, if one studies his later measures keeping this factor in mind, Aurangzeb as a ruler begins to appear like a natural progression upon Akbar, Jahangir, and Shahjahan. Athar Ali writes that Aurangzeb took to emphasising the 'Islamic character of the Empire' and inaugurated a new religious policy 'intended to create a religious halo around the imperial crown' when he was increasingly beleaguered—the reckless policy of expansion begun in 1659 had proved a complete failure while there were many rebellions by Jats, Satnamis, Yusufzais, Afridis, etc.[141] He adopted a 'discriminatory policy' against the Hindus to 'associate the Muslim orthodoxy as closely as possible with the Empire'.[142] That is why he re-imposed the *jizyā* (abolished by Akbar in his 'enlightened' phase) and began 'progressively shutting out' the Rajputs from the nobility.[143] This was so that he could have *jāgirs* to offer to his Muslim nobility 'in order to rally them more firmly behind his throne'.[144] Satish Chandra, too, avers that the reinstitution of the *jizyā* and the Rajput wars ought to be seen as attempts by Aurangzeb to rally

141 *The Mughal Nobility Under Aurangzeb* (New Delhi: OUP, 2001), p.98

142 Ibid., p.99.

143 Ibid.

144 Ibid., p.100.

Muslim opinion behind him when he was facing reverses in the Deccan. However, he argues that Aurangzeb was not pursuing a 'bitterly anti-Hindu policy' since the number of Hindus in the Mughal nobility rose in the latter part of his reign.[145] Superficially seen, this is true. Overall, the number of Hindus in the nobility did rise during his reign, but this was due to the influx of the Marathas. They had not been 'recruited to the service on account of a policy of religious tolerance, but had practically forced their way in'.[146]

It appears that the Mughal ruling class could be complicit with the Mughal Emperor in culturally constraining the non-Muslims, despite being privy to relatively enlightened viewpoints. For example, the Mughal elites were familiar with the ideas of Khwaja Nasir al-Din Tusi, a thirteenth century Persian polymath. In the *Akhlāq-I Nasiri*, a text that Tusi authored, the ideal ruler was imagined as one who would harmonize the conflicting interests of diverse social and religious groups in the state.[147] Tusi inspired many later thinkers. His conception of Muslim kingship remained the ideal in later *Akhlāq* texts.[148] The intellectual tradition that Tusi inspired emphasised the maintenance of balance in society, and not the stamping out of 'infidelity and idolatry'. [149] The texts composed in emulation of Tusi evaluated a ruler and his concern for justice in light of

145 'Jizyah and the State in India during the Seventeenth Century' in *Essays on Medieval Indian History*, pp.319-320.

146 *The Mughal Nobility Under Aurangzeb,* p.32.

147 *The Languages of Political Islam in India*, p.49.

148 Ibid., p.57.

149 Ibid., p.59.

the reason (*aql*) and 'not any religious code'. [150] Tusi, if not his emulators, had found widespread favour among those who ran the Mughal state. Muzaffar Alam informs us that Tusi's *Akhlāq* 'was among the most favoured readings of the Mughal political elites'.[151] But were Tusi's ideas imbibed and put into practice as well? Well, not quite. Despite their familiarity with Tusi's *Akhlāq*, we learn, the office bearers in the Mughal realm were not very broad-minded in religious matters. Muzaffar Alam acknowledges that it will be a 'travesty of the facts' to claim that they 'generally believed in, and practised, religious tolerance'.[152]

Like its predecessor, the Delhi Sultanate, the language that the Mughal state was partial to was Persian. In fact, one could term the Mughal state extravagantly 'Persophilic'. Though the Mughals were Chaghatay Turks and Babar wrote his autobiography in Turkish, 'it was not Turkish but Persian which came to symbolize Mughal triumph in India'.[153] In simple language, Persian was the language of power in the Mughal domains and was said to have 'emerged as the language of the king, the royal household and the high Mughal elite'.[154] The fact that Persian was associated with the conquerors who had preceded them might have been a reason why it was so valued by the Mughals. As we observe, Persian had originally come to flourish 'in Delhi and beyond, in the wake of the Turkish

150 Ibid., p.59.
151 Ibid., p.61.
152 Ibid., p.75.
153 *The Languages of Political Islam in India*, p.123.
154 Ibid., p.127.

conquest of north India,'[155] that is, upon the establishment of the Delhi Sultanate. Apparently, the cultural vision of this Persian, on account of the Turks who spoke it, was oriented towards the lands beyond India. This was since the Turks considered their Indian conquests parts of the 'Perso-Islamic world, in precisely the same way as Transoxiana, Ghazna, and Ghur'.[156] Akbar, the greatest Mughal ruler, appears to have been similarly infatuated with the 'Perso-Islamic world'. He, for instance, took an 'unusual interest in promoting social, cultural, and intellectual contacts with Iran'.[157] As a result, Mughal India gravitated towards Iran culturally[158] and Persian poetry flowered under the sunny Indian skies. Aziz Ahmad calls the reign of Akbar 'the golden age of Persian poetry in India'.[159] In the meantime, many Iranian and Central Asian immigrants were drawn towards India; among them, one could count princes, noblemen, and men of learning.[160] These immigrants further diffused and 'lent strength' to Indian Perso-Turkic culture. It seems that, besides being its bearers, they also served as its benchmark, for we are told that they caused the native-born courtiers to develop an inferiority complex. These immigrants seem to have been looked upon as cultural archetypes of sorts and were widely emulated—due to them,

155 Ibid., p.117.
156 Ibid., p.118
157 Ibid., p.124.
158 Ibid., p.125.
159 *An Intellectual History of Islam in India*, p.76.
160 *The Languages of Political Islam in India*, pp.143-144.

the preferred high culture among Indian Muslims was Perso-Turkic.[161]

Akbar also made Persian the language of administration at all levels.[162] Probably, the cultural power expressed by Persian was a reason why he chose to do so. Redounding further to its status, the Persian language even 'acquired a kind of religious sanctity among Muslims'.[163] One need not imagine that the 'Islamic' status of Persian was a cultural phenomenon only among the lower-status Muslims who might have been in awe of it. The literate elite too imagined Persian as a 'Muslim tongue'. For example, we learn that Jamat al-Din Inju, the author of the Persian lexicon *Farhang-i Jahāngiri*, dwelt 'at length on the point that Persian, together with Arabic, was the language of Islam'.[164] Anecdotal evidence suggests that the Mughal emperors were acutely conscious of the status and cultural power that Persian communicated. A language widely spoken and understood in the Mughal Empire was Hindavi, but it obviously lacked the glamour of Persian. Nor was it identified as a 'language of Islam'. That is probably why we see that a puritanical ruler like Aurangzeb, though he knew Hindavi, was not very keen on using it. Muzaffar Alam tells us that he 'used Hindavi only when he talked with an Indian who knew no Persian, or who had poor knowledge of the language—and

161 Ibid., p.144.
162 Ibid., p.128.
163 Ibid., p.132.
164 Ibid., pp.132-133.

even this only when it was unavoidable'.[165]

The Mughal Empire did produce a large crop of Persian literate non-Muslims. A lot of Hindus from the traditional literate castes, Brahmans, Kayasthas, and Khatris, for example, did take to the language. But since Persian, as we have seen above, carried a charge of political and cultural power that distinctly belonged to the Islamicate paradigm, the Persian literate non-Muslims, perhaps, ought not to be seen as instances of cultural 'syncretism'. To our eyes, it appears that Persian was unable to provide full citizenship to non-Muslims. First, they must have had to conform to aesthetic standards emanating beyond the borders of India, due to the language's specific geo-cultural orientation. Secondly, since Persian was considered the 'language of Islam,' no matter how much felicity they acquired in it, they, very likely, could never be its true owners. Besides, it seems, making a purely expedient choice to equip himself for positions in a political order that used Persian, the Persian literate non-Muslim was also visibly suffering a fate of cultural subordination.

Like the Delhi Sultanate, the Mughal state closely associated itself with the spiritual charisma of the Sufis. The Mughal emperors were devotees of the Chishti Sufi Shaikhs to the extent that we have Richard Eaton postulating a 'Mughal Chishti partnership'.[166] After setting foot in Delhi, Babur had prayed at the shrine of the Chishti Shaikh, Bakhtiyar Kaki.

165 Ibid., p.148.

166 *Temple Desecration and Muslims States in Medieval India*, p.28.

His brother-in-law, on the other hand, rebuilt the tomb of Nizam al-Din Auliya.[167] Akbar later constructed his father's tomb near this site. He also chose the hospice-site of Salim Chishti for his new capital, Fatehpur Sikri. Jahangir and Shah Jahan constructed 'gates and other buildings at or near the foundational Chishti shrine at Ajmer…'[168] 'The Mughal dynasty, thus,' writes Eaton, 'vigorously patronised the order of Chishti Shaikhs' believing that their blessings underpinned their worldly success'.[169]

Could one term the Mughal rulers (and their predecessors, the rulers of the Delhi Sultanate) 'syncretic' in their outlook due to their penchant for the Sufis? Well, the Sufis could indeed be sympathetic towards non-Muslim religiosity. They, for example, could approach Hindu 'cults and creeds' with an attitude of 'understanding and admiration'. [170] This was because of the Sufi doctrine of *wahdāt al-wajud* (Unity of Being) which inspired a certain amount of catholicity towards the non-Muslims. The Sufis, thus, even adopted some of their practices and ideas demonstrating their ability for 'religious synthesis and cultural amalgam'.[171] But this does not mean that the Sufis were not interested in bringing the non-Muslim into the fold of Islam. Like the Muslim theologians,

167 Ibid., pp.26-27.

168 Ibid., p.27.

169 Ibid.

170 *The Languages of Political Islam in India*, p.82.

171 Ibid., p.91.

the dissemination and consolidation of Islamic power in the lands that the Muslims had conquered was a concern for the Sufis.[172] Indeed, the Sufis believed in the finality of the Islamic revelation and could assert as much. Sufi catholicity towards non-Muslims was, as a result, not limitless, it was very circumscribed indeed. The Sufis could not 'completely free themselves from the hegemony of orthodox, juristic Islam'.[173] A very good example of this inability would be Shaikh Ahmad Sirhindi of the Naqshbandi Sufi order. According to S. Nurul Hasan, his life's mission was to establish the supremacy of the *shari'ā*—he even wrote a letter to Jahangir emphasising that its propagation depended on him.[174] Besides, Shaikh Sirhindi carried out his puritanical propaganda in the Mughal army and administration.[175] Jahangir was alarmed and eventually had the Shaikh imprisoned for a while in 1619, probably because he was getting out of hand. Shaikh Sirhindi was not so unusual, after all, since we come across Sufis who were these dauntless, sword-bearing champions of Islam in the legends. An example would be the Sufi Ghazi Mian, whose grave was venerated by Hindus and Muslims alike. According to the tales that were told about him, Ghazi Mian was a Ghaznavid army commander who had waged jihad against the Hindu rulers.[176] So, individual

172 Ibid., p.88.

173 Ibid., p.161.

174 S. Nurul Hasan, 'Shaikh Ahmad Sirhindi and Mughal Politics' in *Religion, State and Society in Medieval India*, pp.92-93.

175 Ibid., p.97.

176 *The Languages of Political Islam in India*, p.158.

Mughal rulers having their Islamic piety informed by the Sufi outlook very likely did not mean that they stopped viewing the non-Muslims as 'others' who signified fundamental cultural differences.

The Mughal Empire, we may argue based on the foregoing, projected power using almost the same symbolic, or cultural, tropes as the Delhi Sultanate. Notions of sovereignty and royal authority in the Mughal Empire hearkened to Islam as a moral ideal, Mughal sovereigns curtailed the cultural displays of the non-Muslims, and, like the Delhi Sultanate, the Mughal Empire was 'Persophilic' and associated itself with the spiritual charisma of Sufis. The Mughal Empire, thus, was an 'Islamicate' state form, or culture-power formation, in every sense. Having been extremely capable and potent as a culture-power formation for about one hundred and fifty years (1556-1707), the Mughal Empire left two crucial imprints on North India—its political and geographical core. First, it culturally shaped an entire society, the North Indian *ashrāf*. The *ashrāf* were bearers of the Islamicate cultural forms and practices and can truly be said to be the inheritors of the cultural legacy of the Mughal Empire. Secondly, the Mughal Empire created Islamicate cultural spaces all over North India through the *ashrāf*. These were the *qasbās*. The *ashrāf* were based in the *qasbās* and culturally dominated them, generating their distinctly 'Islamicate' identity. One could say that they replicated in the *qasbāti* space the specific alliance of culture and power that the Mughal Empire manifested. Let us now, in the remainder of this chapter, turn our attention to the *ashrāf* and the *qasbās* and assess them, respectively, as an 'Islamicate' society and cultural space.

THE ASHRĀF AND THE 'ISLAMICATE' LEGACY – THE INDO-MUSLIM ELITE AND THEIR CULTURE

Ashrāf is the plural of *sharif*. Typically, Muslims claiming the *sharif* status also claimed foreign ancestry; it made them 'noble'. Thus, *ashrāf* lineages commonly traced their origins to Arabia, Iran, Afghanistan, or Turkey. Being a literate elite, the *ashrāf* were very important to the functioning of the Mughal Empire, forming its transferrable bureaucracy. As David Lelyveld writes, the 'Mughal administrative system rested on an ability to move such people [*ashrāf*] around from place to place'.[177] This fact lent them an aura of power and exclusivity. The association of the *ashrāf* with the Mughal Empire linked them with a history of the 'conquest of and rule over South Asia and its native-born locals'.[178] In their subjective perception too, they were the ruling race, this was the 'well-defined vision of themselves' that they shared.[179] The *ashrāf* had 'come from abroad to rule; the wielding of power was their birthright'.[180]

177 *Aligarh's First Generation. Muslim Solidarity in British India* (New Delhi: OUP, 1996), p.30.

178 Richard Kurin, 'The Culture of Ethnicity in Pakistan' in Katherine P. Ewing, ed., *Sharī'at and Ambiguity in South Asian Islam*, (Berkeley: University of California Press, 1988), p.220.

179 Francis Robinson, 'Perso-Islamic Culture in India from the Seventeenth to the Early Twentieth Century' in *The 'Ulama' of Farangi Mahall and Islamic Culture in South Asia* (Permanent Black, 2001), p.11.

180 Ibid.

The culture that the *ashrāf* espoused and projected, from our point of view,[181] was very 'Islamicate'. One of the foundations of this culture was the 'Persian language and the literature that it expressed'.[182] The *ashrāf* were introduced to Persian when still children, in some local *maktab*.[183] This is understandable, on account of the close relationship that the *ashrāf* had with the Mughal state which was, as we saw above, extremely 'Persophilic'. Literacy in the Persian language must have greatly buttressed the *ashrāf's* aura of power, both in a cultural and worldly sense. This is because, as Muzaffar Alam informs us, the 'long association of the Mughals, and of their supporters and successors, with Persian in the fields of political and military management created a memory of the language as an instrument of conquest'.[184]

Like the 'Persophilic' Mughal state, the *ashrāf* too, through their cultivation of Persian, were oriented towards the 'Islamicate' geo-cultural space. Francis Robinson, for example, points out that nearly 'all the books, commentaries, and the supercommentaries normally used in teaching [Persian] had been written in Iran or Central Asia between 1100 and

---

181 Francis Robinson calls it 'Perso-Islamic'.

182 'Perso-Islamic Culture in India from the Seventeenth to the Early Twentieth Century' in *The 'Ulama' of Farangi Mahall and Islamic Culture in South Asia*, p.13.

183 *Aligarh's First Generation*, p.51.

184 *The Languages of Political Islam in India*, p.134.

1600'.[185] Looking beyond India culturally, the *ashrāf* seem to have tried hard to psychologically sequester themselves from their immediate cultural and social vicinity. They loved to recite the poetry of Rumi and Hafiz, while their own Persian language poetic output was 'remarkable for a complete rejection of Indian life and landscape…'[186] This tendency, very likely, emerged from the *ashrāf* self-perception of being a conquering people and their status as a proud governing elite.[187] By deliberately ignoring its immediate geographical context, it seems, the *ashrāf* authored 'Persian literary tradition in India' expressing a 'wish to distance itself from the polluting influence of the subject peoples'.[188]

Along with Persian, an integral part of the *ashrāf* lifeworld was a scriptural knowledge of Islam. As it appears, *ashrāf* society hearkened to Islam as a moral ideal just as much as the Mughal sovereigns had once done. The *ashrāf* were introduced to scriptural Islam very early in their lives. Studying the Quran was essential to the education of a *sharif* child; it might be done at home under a male or female tutor (depending on the child's gender), or the reciter of a public mosque. [189] Often, *ashrāf* children would be taught Arabic grammar and literature

185 'Perso-Islamic Culture in India from the Seventeenth to the Early Twentieth Century' in *The 'Ulama' of Farangi Mahall and Islamic Culture in South Asia*, p.17.

186 Ibid.

187 Ibid., p.18.

188 Ibid., p.17.

189 *Aligarh's First Generation*, p.50.

as well.[190] The *ashrāf* were, thus, carriers of 'formal' Islamic knowledge, but they did not ignore the 'mystical,' or Sufi traditions of Islam either.[191]

Another language that the *ashrāf* had a penchant for was Urdu, perhaps because it assumed a pronouncedly 'Persianate' character at a point in its development. By the time the British were replacing the Mughals as the rulers, Urdu had become the language of the literate Muslims all over the Subcontinent.[192] The *ashrāf 's* cultivation of Urdu is again vital from our point of view since some of its originary history was closely linked to that of the Mughal Empire. Urdu, very likely, had had its beginnings in Punjab following its Ghaznavid conquest. The Muslim ruling class of the Ghaznavid state, as well as its soldiers, acquired Eastern Punjabi to communicate with the local population and 'impregnated' it with a large number of Persian words. This hybrid language arrived in Delhi from Punjab after the Ghurid conquest of the city. Urdu was then conveyed to the Deccan by the armies of 'Ala-ad-din Khalji and Muhammad bin-Tughlaq where it grew to be a 'literary dialect'.[193] Later, Urdu truly came of age in the Deccan Sultanates of Golconda and Bijapur.[194] These had emerged in the sixteenth century upon the collapse of the Bahmani Sultanate. At the same time, Urdu

190 Ibid., p.52.

191 'Perso-Islamic Culture in India from the Seventeenth to the Early Twentieth Century' in *The 'Ulama' of Farangi Mahall and Islamic Culture in South Asia*, p.13.

192 *Aligarh's First Generation*, p.15.

193 *An Intellectual History of Islam in India*, p.92.

194 Ibid., p.95.

continued to develop in Delhi. We see that it was called 'Urdu-yi mu'alla,' or the language of the exalted camp, in the second half of the seventeenth century.[195] This, we speculate, could have been because Urdu was the preferred argot in the Mughal army. After the Deccan kingdoms were completely annexed by Aurangzeb, there was a drastic change in Urdu 'in the direction of greater Persianization…'[196] There, thus, came into existence a highly Persianized imperial Urdu.[197] At the beginning of the eighteenth century, a number of *mansabdārs*, members of the Mughal aristocracy based in Delhi, had taken to Urdu verse, or *rikhtā*.[198] Some of these poets, as named by Aziz Ahmad, are Siraj-ad-din 'Ali Khan Arzu, Shah Hatim, Sharaf-ad-din Madmun, and Muhammad Shakir Naji.[199] Perhaps, these pioneers of Urdu verse inspired Mirza Rafi Sawda (1713-81) and Mir Taqi Mir (1733-1810), the two most well-known Urdu poets that Delhi produced in the eighteenth century. It was also a time, it seems to us, when Urdu was clearly differentiated from Hindi, as it was deliberately purged of Sanskrit words.[200] Thus, though not officially endorsed by the Mughal Empire, Urdu was, nevertheless, a part of its history. This makes it an aspect of the culture-power formation that was the Mughal Empire. As a matter of fact, Alok Rai writes that, upon the

195 Ibid., p.91.

196 Amrit Rai, *A House Divided. The Origin and Development of Hindi/Hindavi* (Delhi: OUP, 1984), p.239.

197 Ibid., p.240

198 *An Intellectual History of Islam in India*, p.97.

199 Ibid.

200 *A House Divided,* p.246.

ascension of Shah Alam in 1772, Urdu became 'nominally' the language of power.[201] Hence, along with Persian, Urdu was a significant appendage to the *ashrāf's* status.

The spatial setting of *ashrāf* culture and lifeworld was the *qasbā*, a settlement midway between a village and a town. In the Gangetic valley, *qasbās* were 'clustered in the upper Doab and western part of Awadh'.[202] The *ashrāf*, whether soldiers, administrators, scholars, or theologians, lived in *qasbās* 'as aggregates of sub-communities which were often bound together by tight marriage partnerships'. [203] The histories of the *qasbās* seem to have been intrinsically tied to that of the *ashrāf* since, according to C.A. Bayly, 'the slow growth of power of Muslim service families parallelly formed *qasbāti* society'.[204] Islam, as a form of piety and devotion, determined the ethos of the *qasbā* creating 'a shared common culture, a common order of life, and a common disposition of mind'.[205] Thus, rituals and ceremonials of popular Islam such as '*milads* (celebrations of the Prophet's birthday), Muharram observances, the *urs* (the death anniversary of a saint), and *fatiha* (literally, "the opening," the first chapter of the Koran)'[206] were a major

201 *Hindi Nationalism* (Hyderabad: Orient BlackSwan, 2001 [Reprinted 2002, 2007, 2018]), p.74.

202 C.A. Bayly, *Rulers, Townsmen and Bazaars* (OUP: New Delhi, 2014 [Second Impression]), p.423.

203 *From Pluralism to Separatism. Qasbas in Colonial Awadh* (New Delhi: OUP, 2012 [Second Impression]), p.14

204 *Rulers, Townsmen and Bazaars*, p.424.

205 Ibid., 23.

206 Ibid., p.21.

influence on *qasbāti* life. The *qasbā* was, thus, a clearly Islamicate cultural space; all the more because the Mughal Empire's decline had made some qasbas 'the involuntary heirs of the once-powerful Indo-Persian culture'.[207] This was to the extent that, we gather from Mushirul Hasan, the *qasbā* was 'less of "a geographical expression" and more of a cultural and religious unit with a clear Indo-Persian identity—one with a widely shared and recognised cultural traits and patterned behaviour'.[208] We believe this was because the *qasbās* were a spatial setting dominated by the *ashrāf*. Further, we see that, just as the Mughal imperium, many *qasbās* were associated with the spiritual charisma of Sufis. Amroha was known for the '*dargahs* of Saiyyid Sharfuddin Shah Vilayat, Mirza Qazi Saiyyid Abdul Latif, and Sheikh Abdul Majid'. Bilgram too 'attained eminence' due to some *dargāhs*. Again, Rudauli had been the home of 'prominent Sufis, notably Sheikh Ahmad Abdul Haq (d. 1434), or Makhdoom Saheb'.[209] The tombs of Muslim holy men formed the 'moral center' of the *qasbās*.[210]

To what extent did *ashrāf* society interact with the non-elite Muslims resident in the *qasbās*? Polite mingling and formal social intercourse between the two groups can be frankly ruled out. But, of course, the *ashrāf* came into social contact with the latter as they provided them with various services. Further,

207 Ibid., p.17.
208 Ibid., pp.15-16.
209 Ibid., p.13.
210 *Rulers, Townsmen and Bazaars*, p.423.

we think that there is sufficient reason to believe that the 'Islamicate' high culture professed by the *ashrāf,* along with the fact that they were the service elite of the Mughal Empire, made the non-elite Muslims look up to them. Especially because we observe that the average Muslim emotionally identified with the Mughal state, imagining it to be 'his own'. David Lelyveld writes of how, in 1844, a British official named W. H. Sleeman reported that 'Muslims in general identified with the Mughal dynasty, longed for its restoration, and conceived of themselves as the former ruling class'.[211] 'To such people,' Lelyveld adds, 'Mughal rule was Muslim rule…'[212] They were the sort of people 'who assumed that being Muslim entailed a special relationship to the ruling power'.[213]

The fact that the non-elite Muslims very likely looked up to the *ashrāf,* could have implications for the lives of the non-Muslim inhabitants of the *qasbās*. There was, as it seems, always a possibility the non-elite Muslims might spontaneously restrict the cultural displays of the non-Muslims on behalf of the *ashrāf.* Thus, another way in which the *ashrāf* dominated *qasbās* were redolent of the Mughal imperium was that their non-Muslim residents might be forcefully kept from constructing their places of worship. We have this anecdote related by Gyanendra Pandey in his book, *The Construction of Communalism in Colonial North India,* about how some Muslims

211 *Aligarh's First Generation. Muslim Solidarity in British India* (New Delhi: OUP, 1996), p.32.

212 Ibid., p.33.

213 Ibid., p.33.

in a *qasbā* in U.P sought to keep a Hindu moneylender from constructing a temple. In 1877, the Muslims of Mubarakpur discovered that one Manohardas had built a Śivālayā in the compound of his house. They were angry at this and reported the matter to the police. When produced before the magistrate, poor Manohardas argued that,

> …the Muslims of Mubarakpur built mosques and other places of worship wherever they lived, without objection from any source; that no more than five or seven months ago, Faqir Kunjra had erected a masjid close to a place that was sacred to the Hindus and "we did not object". Yet the Muslims wished to destroy the small shivalaya that he had built inside his own house; this was nothing but "a show of power and tyranny". To this, Muslim leaders replied that Faqir Kunjra had built his masjid with the permission of "us zamindars"; all the zamindars of Mubarakpur were Muslims, none Hindu—so what right had the Hindus to object or allow?[214]

In so many words, we might say that Manohardas was kept from constructing a temple by the spontaneous and active collusion of the non-elite Muslims of Mubarakpur and the *ashrāf*. The Muslims who reported Manohardas's temple to the police, we guess, were commoners—somehow, it is hard to imagine the *ashrāf* stepping up to do this. However, when

214 *The Construction of Communalism in Colonial North India* (New Delhi: OUP, 2006), p.132.

the matter eventually came up before the magistrate, it is the *ashrāf* (the likely social identity of these 'zamindars') who led from the front and presented arguments against Manohardas's right to establish a shrine for his deity. As these *ashrāf* saw the situation, a Hindu money lender could not construct a temple, even in his own courtyard, simply because they dominated the *qasbā* as zamindars; there was no doubt in their minds that their supremacy was coterminous with the supremacy of Islam in that spatial setting. This is also why they would not hinder an apparently ordinary Muslim like Faqir Kunjra from constructing a mosque in the same locality. The whole affair seems to demonstrate how the *ashrāf* enforced an 'Islamicate' cultural ambience in the *qasbās* with the non-elite Muslims as their acolytes. The *ashrāf*, one infers, were the natural leaders of Indian Muslim society—they commanded a spontaneous and willing following in its midst. This is the primary reason why we have chosen to refer to them as the 'Indo-Muslim elite'. We do not necessarily mean that the *ashrāf* were Indianized in culture, only that they seem to have exercised a natural hegemony and cultural leadership in Indian Muslim society in general.

THREATS TO THE INDO-MUSLIM ELITE

The Manohardas episode notwithstanding, as we shall see in the next chapter, the Indo-Muslim elite wsere rapidly ceasing to be a privileged and dominant minority in the nineteenth century. Firstly, they were threatened in the administrative roles they discharged, as well as in their position as land controllers, and fell on relatively bad days. Secondly, they ceased to dominate the urban spaces they inhabited and no longer set its cultural register. Eventually, maybe taking an expedient view of their situation, the Indo-Muslim elite sought to make peace, or establish some sort of *modus vivendi*, with colonial rule through the hybrid seminary at Deoband and the 'vernacular' modernity it embodied. Later, as they could not anymore naturally expect government employment due to their 'breeding' alone, they launched a rather awkward project of Western-inspired Islamic modernity in the form of the college at Aligarh. This institution was also meant to be a clearer enunciation of their and broader Indian Muslim society's reconciliation with British rule. Finally, the outbreak of cultural conflicts, as Hindus increasingly asserted their cultural symbols against the backdrop of the introduction of local self-government, jeopardized the broad social hegemony of the 'Islamicate' cultural paradigm that the Indo-Muslim elite represented. The only thing that unambiguously worked in their favour in the nineteenth century was perhaps the puritanical reforms they undertook—these, it seems, further bulwarked their leadership position in Indian Muslim society as they made the non-elite Muslims very conscious of their Islamic identity.

THE INDO-MUSLIM ELITE IN THE NINETEENTH CENTURY

INSECURITIES, CULTURAL CONFLICTS, THE 'ISLAMICATE' IMPERILED

AN INSECURE AGE

WE FIND THE Mughal administration in a rather tumbledown state in the major urban centres of North India at the turn of the nineteenth century. This must mean that the Indo-Muslim elite, or the *ashrāf*, were witnessing a major erosion of their authority. They were, after all, as we saw in the previous chapter, the administrative vanguard of the Mughal Empire. As seen by C.A. Bayly, the 'city-wide institutions' of 'Indo-Islamic tradition' were now in decline.[1] Apparently, this was because the officials who discharged the police and judicial functions of the Mughal urban administration, namely, the *kotwāl* and the *kāzi*, had been losing their moral authority

---

1 *Rulers, Townsmen and Bazaars. North Indian Society in the Age of British Expansion. 1770-1870* (OUP: New Delhi, 2014 [Second Impression]), p.368.

for the preceding many decades. For example, when disputes arose over the Gyanvapi Mosque in Benaras and the Sulaiman Mosque in Ayodhya, some Muslim 'law officers' supported their coreligionists and 'forfeited the confidence of Hindu residents'.[2] While the *kotwāl* and the *kāzi* lost credibility, the Hindu elite grew proportionately powerful. As C.A. Bayly writes, the 'princelings of the new Hindu house of Benaras began to assert their jurisdiction over bazaars…'[3]

The East India Company (EIC) too, enjoying *diwāni* rights since 1764, was growing concomitantly powerful and undermined the institutional symbols of Muslim power. After Lord Cornwallis' reorganisation of the EIC administration, it became all too clear 'that Muslims would not be the subordinate partners of the British, but merely subordinates'.[4] In 1790, Cornwallis abolished the post of *nāib nizām*, dismissed Muslim judges, and reconstituted the *nizāmat adālat* with Europeans after moving it to Calcutta.[5] In the words of Bayly, the utilitarian approach of British magistrates and law courts abolished whole areas of the moral and social jurisdiction of the *kotwāls, kāzis,* and *muftis.*[6] In the face of the relentless approach of a new regime of power, these old representatives of Mughal authority became acutely aware that Muslims and Islam no more ruled the land. We learn that when the British

2 Ibid., p.377.

3 Ibid.

4 *The Muslims of British India* (CUP, 1972), p.37.

5 Ibid.

6 *Rulers, Townsmen and Bazaars*, p.379.

levied a 'house tax' in Bareilly in 1816, the *mufti* of the city saw it as the imposition of a sort of *jizyā* on Muslims. He was convinced that this 'Christian tax' symbolised the end of Muslim political dominance.[7]

As the Indo-Muslim elite were increasingly hamstrung as administrators, the power equilibrium that hitherto existed between the Hindus and Muslims in North India, it seems, was quickly giving way. This is indicated by the frequent outbreaks of communal clashes over the 1820s and 30s. We learn from Bayly that Hindus and Muslims came to blows at Benares (1809-15), Koil (1820), Moradabad, Sambhal, Kashipur, Shahjahanpur (1837), Bareilly, Kanpur, and Allahabad (1837-52).[8] The relative eclipse and weakening of the authority of the *kāzis, muftis,* and *kotwāls*—representatives of the old regime—was the very likely cause behind these outbreaks of violence. According to Bayly, the European police and magistracy 'played one off against the other' while reducing their influence.[9] As the old Muslim service elite declined, new social groups ascended and filled the power vacuum left by them. Bayly gives examples of Agarwal Banias around Kanpur and Chaubes in the Mathura region.[10] There were now, in the North Indian urban context, significant numbers of upwardly mobile Hindus who were culturally assertive. Bayly relates how, once in 1838, the Hindu

7 Ibid., p.394.
8 Ibid., p.406.
9 Ibid., p.407.
10 Ibid., p.409.

commercial community in Rewari, a town north of Delhi, sought to coerce the local Muslims to give up the slaughter of animals by conducting a *hartāl* and denying them food.[11] In Delhi itself, we are told, 'sporadic communal violence' occurred in the 'early colonial period' on account of the growing power and wealth of the merchant communities.[12] The Islamicate character of the erstwhile centres of Muslim power was clearly under a concerted assault. The old Indo-Muslim elite who left their stamp on these places through the exercise of political and administrative power were now being challenged, even physically threatened, by the increasingly aggressive votaries and representatives of the Hindu way of life.

Just as in judicial and police administration, it appears that the Indo-Muslim elite often found the going difficult as revenue intermediaries and a landed class after the onset of Company rule. Peter Hardy writes that the power and influence of the Muslim landlords persisted well into the twentieth century[13] in the North-Western Provinces (today's western Uttar Pradesh). This is, no doubt, a broad reality (as we shall see below). However, it is also true that, in many cases, Muslims suffered significant setbacks as 'land controllers' under the new administration. This, ironically, might be because they preponderated in this role in the Gangetic plains. Take, for instance, the anti-

11 Ibid.

12 Ibid., p.410.

13 *The Muslims of British India*, p.39.

tāluqdāri settlements of Thomason and Bird that Bayly refers to. These initiatives tried to deprive the *tāluqdārs* of a 'large proportion of their revenue engaging rights'[14] and handed them over to a 'variety of village magnates'.[15] Since Muslims were very numerous as revenue intermediaries in the Gangetic heartland,[16] it seems safe to assume that they were the ones most affected. As a matter of fact, even in Awadh, which did not come under British rule till 1856, Muslims were facing difficulties as revenue intermediaries. Bayly writes that the 'hold' of the small town 'Islamic gentry' over revenue-rights had already weakened before the annexation of Awadh by the British in 1858.[17] When Wajid Ali Shah ruled the realm, for example, the small '*qasbāh* zamindars' were an embattled lot. According to Bayly, both the regime and the rural Rajput clans, in the process of resuscitating their power, were exerting pressure on them.[18] Simultaneous to the reviving vigor of the Hindu landowning castes, it appears, was the rise of Hindu merchant groups. Seemingly, the two groups very effectively challenged the 'Islamicate' character of the Awadhi *qasbās*. Bayly mentions how in Sandila, a town in the erstwhile kingdom of Awadh, 'not a single Hindu temple' could be built till the 'last quarter' of the nineteenth century.[19] Later, however,

14 *Rulers, Townsmen and Bazaars*, p.330.

15 Ibid.

16 Peter Hardy notes that Muslims were 'very numerous' as *tahsildars*, 'or Indian collectors of revenue, at the *tahsil* level' in the North-Western Provinces. See *The Muslims of British India*, p.38.

17 *Rulers, Townsmen and Bazaars*, p.429.

18 Ibid.

19 Ibid., p.433.

as he puts it, 'the reassertion of Hindu tradition was forceful.'[20]

One part of India where the situation of Muslims was unambiguously bad in land and revenue administration was Bengal. There they were not represented in proportion to their numbers in the 'new landlord class'[21] that was created by the Company administration. According to Hardy, the Permanent Settlement meant the 'virtual closing of the door to landlordism to Muslims'.[22] The majority who were engaged by the EIC in Bengal 'for the payment of revenue' were Hindus since they 'were *zamindars* in the Mughal sense or…revenue farmers'.[23] In Western India, in the 'Maratha country' too, Muslims appear to have fared badly as a landed class. Muslim *jāgirdārs* found their *jāgirs* 'under critical scrutiny, detailed inquisition, and with frequent resumption and commutation to pension'.[24]

Thus, we find that the worldly fortunes of the Indo-Muslim elite suffered a perceptible decline under British rule. Nevertheless, let it also be clear that it was only a *relative* decline. In the former centre of Indo-Muslim power, that is, the Gangetic heartland, Muslims continued to be well represented in landownership and government jobs. For example, Francis Robinson writes that Muslims were a 'major landholding group' in the United Provinces along with Hindu Rajputs, Brahmans,

20 Ibid.
21 *The Muslims of British India*, p.39.
22 Ibid., p.43.
23 Ibid.
24 Ibid., p.39.

Banias, and Kayasthas.[25] They also held thirty-five per cent of all government posts in the province in 1882.[26] As far as the upper strata of Indian Muslim society were concerned, the sense of cultural loss and humiliation might have been more galling than any reduction of means. British rule left the Indo-Muslim elite not economically but psychologically insecure. Hardy, for example, writes that a minority (of Indian Muslims) lost 'not a livelihood, but a way of life' due to British rule and that it 'damaged not so much their pockets as their pride'.[27] This sounds very plausible since, as we saw, British rule was emboldening ascendent Hindu groups to challenge the former hegemony of the Indo-Muslim elite in the urban spaces of North India. On the other hand, we find Hardy writing that the British had nothing but scorn for the 'Mughal past and Mughal present,' and put no premium on 'gentility and poetry and those who did not live laborious lives'.[28] In other words, precisely the heritage and lifestyle of the Indo-Muslim elite, or the *ashrāf*.

As the Mughal Empire gradually weakened and withered away, one perceives considerable psychological trauma among the custodians of the spiritual and intellectual heritage of Islam. The Muslim divines and scholars, or the *ulāmā,* another component of Indo-Muslim elite society, felt the loss very

---

25 *Separatism among Indian Muslims. The Politics of the United Provinces' Muslims* (Delhi: OUP, 1994 [Second Impression]), p.17.

26 Ibid., p.23.

27 *The Muslims of British India*, p.49.

28 Ibid., p.50.

sharply as an alien regime replaced the Mughal Empire—it spelt the end of the formal political and cultural paramountcy of Islam in the Indian context. Without a court as its protector and patron, the Indian *ulāmā* became conscious of their responsibility of 'guarding the intellectual heritage' of Islam.[29] The idea bestirred the seminary at Farangi Mahal as well as an individual scholar such as Shah Waliullah (1703-1762) in the eighteenth century. Around the middle of the eighteenth century, the Farangi Mahal *ulāmā* systematised and created an exhaustive curriculum of Islamic education.[30] One assumes that in terms of content it was as orthodox as it could get. This is because the Farangi Mahallis, as Francis Robinson calls them, were so puritanically inclined as to live in deliberate ignorance of the preponderate Indian religion. They had, since their arrival in Lucknow in the late seventeenth century, 'been able to largely ignore the Hindu world about them'.[31] The Farangi Mahallis, thus, lived in a sequestered world of their own and sought to serve Islam through a purity of cultural vision and conduct. Shah Waliullah, on the other hand, understood and sought to serve, the interests of Islam politically. He was concerned by the absence of both a *khilāfat* and a stable Muslim monarchy in the age. He, we learn, resultantly wrote to multiple Muslim

---

29 Barbara Dally Metcalf, *Islamic Revival in British India, 1860-1900* (Karachi: Royal Book Company, 1989), p.29.

30 Ibid., p.31.

31 Francis Robinson, 'Living Together Separately: The '*Ulama* of Farangi Mahall. *C.* 1700 – *C.* 1950' in Mushirul Hasan and Asim Roy, eds., *Living Together Separately. Cultural India in History and Politics* (New Delhi: OUP, 2005), p.364.

rulers, that of Hyderabad, Rohilkhand, and even Afghanistan, exhorting them to 'take on the required role'[32] (of the leader of the faithful?) Shah Waliullah had envisioned an 'enlightened' Muslim leadership that would be guided by a 'responsible' *ulāmā*.[33] His exhortations to Muslim rulers, unfortunately, bore no fruit.

Barbara D. Metcalf notices two concomitant tendencies among the Indian *ulāmā* in the nineteenth century. First, they focused more on the study of legal codes (*fiqh*) and drafting of legal opinions (*fatwā*) 'for increasing numbers of individual Muslims'.[34] Secondly, several of the *ulāmā* sought to create a 'new Islamic order' through *jihād*.[35] Thus, they attempted to foment military revolt on the borders of the erstwhile Mughal Empire. The resentment of the *ulāmā* is understandable in the light of the fact that the new state, on account of its non-Islamic character, did not prominently accommodate them in its power structure. For instance, what was once 'Muslim law' was turned into 'Anglo-Muhammadan law' in the legal administration of colonial Bengal. In terms of the law of evidence and the way it interpreted offences against the state, Anglo-Muhammadan law, Metcalf writes, was mainly British and not Muslim. Understandably, it was also administered by British officials, though they initially took the help of local scholars.[36]

32 *Islamic Revival in British India*, p.35.
33 Ibid.
34 Ibid., p.46.
35 Ibid., p.47.
36 Ibid., p.49.

Denied a substantial role by the new state, the *ulāmā* withdrew into a reflective mood. Seemingly, the more acute and sensitive among them sought to rediscover their relevance in relation to the community of believers. Shah Abdul Aziz (1746-1824), the eldest son of Shah Waliullah, for example, hoped to 'transform' the lives of Muslims through 'scholarly guidance'.[37] Sayyid Ahmed Barelvi (1786-1831) was a radical. According to Metcalf, his idea was to 'destroy society itself and build it anew on a just and egalitarian basis'.[38] It seems that he wanted to completely refashion Indian Islam in a puritanical mould. Sayyid Ahmed began an ardent campaign to purge Indian Islam of 'abuses' such as invoking the intercession of saints, apostles, imams, martyrs, angels, and fairies along with the keeping of *taziyās* after the fashion of the Shias.[39] He followed up these efforts at reform by launching a *jihād* from the tribal areas of the Northwest. It was initially directed against the Sikh kingdom which he accused of 'interfering with Muslim religious life'.[40] Sayyid Ahmed met his end at the hands of the Sikhs at Balakot in 1831.[41]

Puritanical Islamic reform and militancy had their votaries at the other extremity of India, in Bengal. Haji Shariatullah (1781-1840) and Titu Mir (1782-1831) were exact contemporaries and addressed the Muslim society of rural Bengal. The former

37 Ibid., p.52.
38 Ibid.
39 Ibid., p.57.
40 Ibid., p.61.
41 Ibid., 62.

launched a movement called *farāizi* (from *farz*, Arabic for fundamentals). Its objective was to teach the Bengali Muslims correct Islamic observances, by emphasising the fundamentals of Islam. The extent of Shariatullah's radicalism and abhorrence for British rule was such that he termed Bengal *dār al-harb*, or land of war, where Eid celebrations and Friday prayers were illicit. These could be conducted again by the Muslims of Bengal, thought he, once the land was restored to Muslim rule. Titu Mir led a jacquerie of sorts of Bengali-Muslim peasants against their Hindu zamindars and the colonial state. He too urged his followers to take proper Islamic names and keep beards. He also forbade them from paying the cesses that the Hindu *zamindārs* levied for conducting or sponsoring Hindu religious festivities. Titu was killed in an encounter with the East India Company's troops in 1831.

Rafiuddin Ahmed suggests that the reforming *ulāmā* were seeking to restore the power Muslims had lost in India through a 'return to the primitive purity of Islam'.[42] They attributed the political, social, and economic 'disasters' that Indian Muslims had experienced to their religious degeneration. The *ulāmā,* thus, embarked on a program of the spiritual regeneration of Indian Muslims while also defending Islam against its enemies.[43] Was there any substantial change in Indian Islam in the process? There was, indeed. Peter Hardy writes that the

42 Rafiuddin Ahmed, *The Bengal Muslims. A Quest for Identity. 1871-906* (Delhi: OUP, 1981), p.41.

43 Ibid.

reform movements rejected 'medieval Islam in India in favour of early Islam in Arabia'.[44] By bypassing its medieval intellectual legacy, one might argue hearkening to Francis Robinson, our reformers were seeking to go back to the 'pristine' beginnings of Islam by making 'contact with the Qur'an and Hadith afresh'.[45] They were also attempting to make them 'relevant to the modern world'.[46] This made them, in present day terms, 'activists'. What we ought to be mindful of is that the militant Muslim puritans were not so many sequestered scholars. Nor was their 'reform' a set of intellectual formulations that they quietly arrived at in private. They went out among Indian Muslims and influenced and won followers among them. Thus, Hardy's view that they 'helped to transform Muslim attitudes towards Hindus'[47] seems very reasonable. He observes how the puritan Muslim reformers sought to reform the local elements in Indian Islam such as seeking the intercession of saints, vegetarianism, consulting Brahmins, and dislike of widow remarriage. Their audience, therefore, became aware of 'what they did not share with their non-Muslim neighbours'.[48] They were made to feel, Hardy writes tellingly, that India was their 'habitat' and not home.[49]

44 *The Muslims of British India*, p.59.

45 'Islamic Reform and Modernities in South Asia,' *Modern Asian Studies*, Vol.42, NO. 2/3, Islam in South Asia (Mar.-May, 2008), pp.259-281. P.267.

46 Ibid.

47 *The Muslims of British India*, p.59.

48 Ibid.

49 Ibid.

In terms of cultural practices, thus, Indian Muslim society became, in certain instances, very conscious of its distinctiveness and individuality over the nineteenth century. Further, as it was drawn away from local cults 'towards widely shared [Islamic] practices and symbols,' Francis Robinson thinks, Indian Muslim society was groomed 'for the world of the modern political party and the modern state'.[50] In other words, we might say that, as Indian Muslims were made to give up what was local and 'not Islam' in their lives, they acquired the potential to override the specific conditions of their existence and politically cohere with their coreligionists elsewhere around Islamic 'fundamentals'. Thus, it appears that the reform efforts infused an ideological element into the Indian Muslims' sense of who they were. Equally, if not more importantly, puritanical Islamic reform bred into its audience a legitimate notion of Islamic agency which had to be deployed in the world. Robinson writes that in the 'many manifestations of [Islamic] reform in India' there was a stress on 'personal responsibility before God, as well on the need to act on earth to achieve salvation'.[51] At the same time, Islamic reform emphasised 'human will'. In doing so it was inspired by the notion that 'in the absence of Muslim power' the will of 'each individual Muslim' was to fashion an Islamic society. Post reform, as understood by Robinson, Indian Islam 'was a willed faith, a "protestant" faith, a faith of conscience and conviction'.[52]

50 'Islamic Reform and Modernities in South Asia,' p.275.
51 Ibid., p.264.
52 Ibid., p.269.

In total, we might say, Indian Islam stood transformed in the nineteenth century due to a number of social and cultural re-engineering efforts undertaken by the Indo-Muslim elite—even the peasant radical Titu Mir claimed Arab ancestry, while the rest of the reformers quite obviously came from the upper strata of Indian Muslim society.[53] The Indo-Muslim elite, thus, it seems to us, laid the foundations of a more self-reflexive, socially and culturally cohesive, and politically and ideologically motivated Indian Muslim society in the period under our consideration. They also, in the process, we suggest, assumed a conspicuous leadership position in this society.

Haji Shariatullah and Titu Mir were the last of the Indian Muslims who sought to overthrow the new political dispensation by instigating armed insurgent action against it. Thereafter, it seems, the Indian Muslim leadership began to seek a *modus vivendi* of sorts with British rule. Instead of expending energies on politically opposing the British, the Indo-Muslim elite now focused on intellectually revivifying Indian Islam. A feasible template for it, interestingly, was provided by the colonial state. While Titu Mir was developing into a religiously motivated insurgent in faraway Bengal, the

---

53 These reformers were very obviously the elites of Indian Muslim society, as the information available about them indicates. Shah Waliullah clearly seems to have been from an *ashrāf* background. His father had served under Aurangzeb and been one of the compilers of the *Fatawā-e- Ālamgiri.* We assume that Sayyid Ahmed Barelvi too came from *ashrāf* society, as his family had apparently migrated to India back in the thirteenth century. Haji Shariatullah was not *ashrāf,* it seems, but his family were *taluqdārs* and, one assumes, of considerable means.

colonial administration founded the Delhi College in 1825. Though a short-lived institution that was wound up after the uprising of 1857, according to Metcalf, it provided the *ulāmā* a model to strengthen 'the organisation of religious education'.[54] Furthermore, by the late nineteenth century, the *ulāmā* were motivated by a 'pervasive concern' to 'maintain Muslim culture and society'.[55] It is claimed that the aftermath of 1857 had been especially harsh for Indian Muslims since they were the chief culprits in the eyes of the colonial administration.[56] Apparently, as the state was so obviously hostile to the Muslims, the *ulāmā* now eliminated the 'political dimension from their thought' and avoided causing offence to their rulers.[57] It seems that they reinvented themselves as a lot that was 'inward-looking and primarily concerned with Islamic quality of individual lives'.[58] The *ulāmā,* thus, made the *madrasāh* the 'institutional basis of their work'.[59] They, one surmises, positioned themselves as guides and preceptors in relation to the community of believers by being the source of the right Islamic education.

The new *madrasāh* that was coming into existence in the second half of the nineteenth century was of a different sort. It was exemplified by the *madrasāh* at Deoband. Metcalf writes that it was modelled on the British institutions whose

54 *Islamic Revival in British India*, p.72.

55 Ibid., p.86.

56 Ibid., p.85.

57 Ibid., 85.

58 Ibid., p.86.

59 Ibid., p.88.

'effectiveness' had been 'witnessed' by the *ulāmā*.[60] Founded in 1867, the objective of this new type of *madrasāh* at Deoband was to train a Muslim religious leadership that would discharge a public role and keep Indian Islam on the path of puritanical reform. The Deoband seminary, informs Metcalf, sought to train an *ulāmā* dedicated to 'reformed Islam' and capable of disseminating their learning as 'prayer leaders, writers, preachers, and teachers'.[61] The curriculum that was followed at Deoband was of course very traditional—its stress was on the study of the Quran, *hadis*, and *fiqh*. Parallelly, the Deoband scholars were made to follow an observant Islamic lifestyle in the traditional sense. Yet, one might say, the seminary at Deoband articulated Indian Islam's first tentative attempts at finding its own 'vernacular' modernity. It followed, for instance, a system of examinations and evaluation very similar to that of the British sort of educational institutions. Deoband's pedagogy too was, in some ways, non-traditional and British inspired. To cite an example, the technique of Arabic instruction that was adopted there was apparently derived from the Delhi College. We see that it was the 'British one of translation into Urdu and from Urdu into Arabic'.[62] By using Urdu as a medium of instruction, the Deoband *madrasāh* was also a contributor to the 'general trend' of the development of 'modern vernaculars'.[63]

---

60 Ibid., p.94.
61 Ibid., p.100.
62 Ibid., p.102.
63 Ibid.

In less than a decade and a half, Deoband had spawned its imitators. By roughly 1880, we learn, 'there were over a dozen schools' which termed themselves 'Deobandi'.[64] It is likely that this was the result of cooperation between the alumni of Deoband.[65] These 'Deobandi' *madrasāhs* spanned the length and breadth of the Indian Subcontinent, located as far afield as Chittagong, Madras, and Peshawar.[66] The Deoband seminary, thus, was being the purveyor of an intensely puritanical variety of Islamic modernity. This is evident in the primary role that the Deobandis had identified for themselves. According to Metcalf, it was one of *mufti*, or 'giving advisory opinion' on Islamic law.[67]

In its early days, most of the students and staff at the Deoband *madrasāh* came from an *ashrāf* background.[68] So did most of the donors.[69] The Deoband *madrasāh*, thus, we are tempted to observe, was an institutional expression of Indo-Muslim elite society. Why were the *ashrāf* sympathetic towards this institution? The 'presence of non-Muslim rulers, new patterns of recruitment to government service, the economic consequences of colonial rule,'[70] we are told, caused them considerable distress. Against all the bleakness, the Deoband

---

64 Ibid., 136.
65 Ibid., p.133.
66 Ibid.
67 Ibid., p.140.
68 Ibid., p.248.
69 Ibid., p.238.
70 Ibid., p.252.

madrasāh, it seems, was a source of psychological comfort for the Indo-Muslim elite. Metcalf argues that it 'offered a formulation of Islam' that was 'very salient to the concerns of the urban *ashrāf*'[71] (perhaps because of its puritanical bent). At the same time, the Deoband *madrasāh* 'provided a modus vivendi with the political situation of the day'.[72]

The Indo-Muslim elite were now seemingly at a turn that they were seeking reconciliation with British rule. A significant reason behind this, one hazards the guess, was that their access to government employment and patronage was imperilled. Earlier, when the Mughal Empire was intact, they could assume that 'being Muslim entailed a special relationship to the ruling power'.[73] The circumstances, it seems, did not change immediately as the colonial administration took root in North India. David Lelyveld writes that 'through most of the nineteenth century'[74] success in government service could be achieved through 'a good maktab education in Persian,' apprenticing oneself under some relative in a government office, and personal ties with important Indians and Englishmen.[75] A Muslim of *sharif* descent, thus, could win government employment by just loitering about and forming connections at the *kachahri,* described by Lelyveld as 'the complex of

71 Ibid., p.252.

72 Ibid., pp.252-253.

73 David Lelyveld, *Aligarh's First Generation. Muslim Solidarity in British India* (New Delhi: OUP, 1996), p.33.

74 Ibid., p.60.

75 Ibid., pp.60-61.

courts and government offices…[marking] any administrative centre'.[76] However, it appears that this informal pathway to government employment, built on 'culture' and 'connections,' was increasingly becoming a thing of the past in the last third of the nineteenth century. The colonial administration was laying down more demanding criteria for those seeking government employment, or even advancement and growth therein. For instance, Lelyveld informs as to how 'some knowledge of English was necessary' for one to get employment at the 'higher levels' of the legal profession or the judicial service after 1865.[77] The demand to replace Urdu with Hindi as the administrative language further threatened the culture of *sharāfat* in government offices in the 1860s.[78] As we shall see below, the agitation in favour of Hindi was partially successful when the Lieutenant Governor of Bengal ruled that Hindi and not Urdu be used in the courts of Bihar in 1871.[79] As their 'breeding' and 'cultivation' did not anymore assure government employment by default, the *ashrāf* had every reason to be worried and actively court the favours of the alien regime.

While the Indo-Muslim elite were getting conciliatory, the British too, on their part, were ready to reassess their attitude towards Indian Muslims at large. The colonial administration had treated them with suspicion since 1857. The chiefly Muslim character of the uprising, apparently, was all too

76 Ibid., p.57.
77 Ibid., p.95.
78 Ibid., p.97.
79 Ibid., p.98.

obvious in the eyes of the British. As Hardy writes, the Muslim troopers of the 3rd Native Cavalry were 'among the first to be provoked into mutiny,' while the Mughal Emperor and his court had not been 'too reluctant' to assume the leadership role assigned to them by mutineers.[80] Thus, after they crushed the rebellion, the British sometimes (not always) penalised the Muslims a lot more than the Hindus. For example, the Hindus who had fled Delhi after its reconquest by the British had to pay ten per cent of the value of their real property as fine if they wished to return. The Muslims, on the other hand, had to pay twenty-five per cent.[81] However, by the 1870s, it appears, the colonial regime had been considering a policy of 'balance and rule between the Hindu and Muslim communities'.[82] For this policy to be feasible, Muslims had to be convinced that they had 'more to gain by collaboration than by opposition'.[83] But were Indian Muslims in a mood to acquiesce to British rule and cooperate with it? It is likely that this question was bothering the Governor-General, Lord Mayo. He, thus, got a Bengal civilian, W.W. Hunter to write a book on it. Hunter did not take long to come up with the rhetorically titled volume *The Indian Musalmans, Are They Bound in Conscience to Rebel Against the Queen?* He opined that not all Muslims were pathologically averse to British rule and looking to rise against it. He thought that the pragmatic Muslims could be won over by the British

80 *Muslims of British India*, p.63.

81 Ibid., p.71.

82 Ibid., p.80.

83 Ibid.

and their sympathies diverted from the seditious elements in their community. Hunter recommended that the government mitigate 'the bitter doctrines of their medieval law' with 'the sober and genial knowledge of the West'.[84] He visualised a scenario in which these Muslims would have 'sufficient acquaintance with their religious code' to command respect in their own community, while also possessing an English training that would secure them 'entry into the lucrative walks of life'.[85] Even though Lord Mayo was assassinated by a Muslim the next year, the colonial administration did not victimize Muslims in any manner. It had, as Hardy writes, decided to 'offer the chalice of reconciliation' to the Muslims of India.[86]

Syed Ahmed Khan (1817-1898), a pedigreed *sharif*, was eager to grab this chalice with both hands. He was greatly invested in reconciling Indian Muslims with British rule and, if necessary, resorted to Muslim jurisprudence for that. He argued, for instance, that Muslims are required to be thankful to just rulers and pointed out how Queen Victoria was ruling India without communal and religious bias. He, thus, concluded that the British are just rulers and Muslims ought to be grateful to them.[87] More significantly, Khan considered the debate as to whether India under the British is *dār al-harb* or *dār al-Islām* unnecessary. As he understood the situation, British ruled India was just that—British India. It was neither

84 Ibid., p.88.

85 Ibid.

86 Ibid., p.92.

87 *The Muslims of British India*, p.112.

dār al-harb nor *dār al-Islām*. Since Muslims enjoyed the security that British rule provided, Khan thought, British India might be termed *dār al-aman* or *dār al-zimma*—'home of security or protection'.[88]

Just as much as he wanted Indian Muslims to accept British rule, Khan wanted them to acquire Western learning and 'reason'. As seen by Hardy, he was calling his co-religionists to 'the strenuous life of free inquiry into what God required of them in the world of the nineteenth century'.[89] Khan, writes Hardy, thought that 'God's guidance for man in earthly society'[90] was not to be fully found in the Quranic revelation. Instead, it had to be 'sought in the immanent revelation of man's reason applying itself to the changing circumstances of man's social existence'.[91] His faith in human reason made him a radical as to how he approached fundamental Islamic concepts and beliefs. As Khan understood, statements pertaining to the attributes of God in the Quran and *hadīth* were allegorical and not meant to be taken literally. He thought the same about the day of judgement and heaven and hell. Satan, in his view, was not a being, 'but the personification of man's lower self'.[92]

In his heterodoxy, Khan strikingly differed from contemporary Muslim intellectuals such as Altaf Hussain Hali (1837-1914) and Shibli Nomani (1857-1914), both of whom

---

88 Ibid., p.113.
89 Ibid., p.101.
90 Ibid., p.100.
91 Ibid.
92 M. Mujeeb, *The Indian Muslims* (New Delhi: Munshiram Manoharlal Publishers Pvt. Ltd., 2017 [Fourth Reprint]), p.450.

(like our reformers above) thought that the salvation of Indian Islam lay in a return to 'purity'. Hali 'berated the existing [Muslim] society' and its decadence and inadequacy. He did so not by comparing it to contemporary Western culture, but the glories of Baghdad and Muslim Spain.[93] Shibli Nomani was similarly infatuated with Islam's past. He did not wish to 'reform Islam with some new criterion, but to revive it from within…'[94] His ambition was to restore Islamic learning in its entirety so that it flowered as it had under the Abbasids in Baghdad.[95]

Syed Ahmed Khan's vision drew inspiration from the West. To bring the light of Western learning and reason to his co-religionists, Khan founded the Translation Society in 1863. He later renamed it the Scientific Society. In a few years' time, Khan had come to think of a 'separate Muslim education movement'.[96] According to Lelyveld, this happened when he visited England for eighteen months in 1869-70.[97] In the early part of his stay in England, Khan authored the pamphlet *Strictures on the Present State of English Education in India*. He observed therein that the system of schools that the British had established in India had failed to achieve both mass education and the 'stimulation of intellectual creativity'.[98] Inquiring into

93 Wilfred Cantwell Smith, *Modern Islam in India. A Social Analysis* (London: Victor Gollancz Ltd., 1946), p.38.

94 Ibid., p.40.

95 Ibid.

96 *Aligarh's First Generation*, p.104.

97 Ibid., pp.104-105.

98 Ibid., p.107.

the bases of British power and achievements, Khan thought that these were, along with technological innovation, 'the diffusion of knowledge and skills to a wide population'.[99] While forming these consequential notions, Khan was also becoming aware of the humiliation of Islam by Europeans. Lelyveld writes that this realisation came to him when he viewed a mural at Versailles depicting the French conquest of Algeria[100] (apparently, he took time off to cross the English Channel and visit France). It seems that the gist of what Khan observed, thought, and concluded while in England was that 'there was a correlation between worldly success and cultural superiority'.[101] Further, his English sojourn, Lelyveld writes, had got him to see religion as a part of social discipline.[102] He, for example, saw that schools in England compulsorily have a chapel and sensed the 'pervasiveness of religious consciousness in Victorian life'.[103] This, we are told, 'prepared him for the confluence of religion and education in his own program of public action'.[104] After his return to India, Khan set about translating his ideas into action. He established the Committee for the Better Diffusion and Advancement of Learning among Muhammadans of India in 1870. By 1872, he had got it to unanimously approve the plan for a 'private Muslim school system that would give

99 Ibid., p.108.
100 Ibid., p.109.
101 Ibid., p.112.
102 Ibid., p.115.
103 Ibid., p.114.
104 Ibid., p.115.

sufficient place to religious practice and instruction'.[105] This eventually led to the establishment of Muhammadan Anglo-Oriental College at Aligarh in 1875.

Unsettled in many ways, Indo-Muslim elite society had now thrown up a unique project of modernity. As we see, it improved upon the project already underway at Deoband. What was being attempted at Aligarh was not the production of a purely 'vernacular' Indo-Islamic modernity, but one that would creatively amalgamate the intellectual offerings of the West into the Indian Muslim lifeworld and reenergise it, while also reconciling it with British rule. What was being attempted at Aligarh, thus, was a thorough 'reboot' of Indian Muslim society. The idea was to invest it with the right skills and attitude so that it may regain its place in the sun that lit the British Indian Empire. The Indo-Muslim elite were now at a crucial juncture when they needed security, stability, and the rulers' goodwill more than anything else, so that the project they had undertaken was not jeopardised. They were in no position to afford a radical political experiment or misadventure.

CULTURAL CONFLICTS–CHALLENGES TO THE 'ISLAMICATE'

Nominally, a Mughal Emperor continued to occupy the throne at the Red Fort in Delhi till 1857. But he wore a 'hollow crown'. He definitely did not rule, and even his reign was illusory to say the least. Mughal sovereignty was without all substantive

105 Ibid., p.119.

content in the nineteenth century. To use a phrase originally coined by Clifford Geertz and later used by Nocholas Dirks in his ethnohistorical study of the South Indian principality of Pudukkottai—the Mughal Empire, though not formally extinguished till 1857, was reduced to being a 'theatre state' by the East India Company. Shah Alam II (r. 1760-1806) onwards, Mughal sovereigns were pensioners of the British. One might say that they were absorbed into a colonial edifice of 'loyalty and subservience'[106] in this capacity, along with numerous talukdars, zamindars, and princes. No matter how much glamor they exuded, or how precious their persons, they belonged, at the end of the day, to the 'gentrified managerial elite' that the British had created as 'a tribute, and a support' to their rule.[107] In plain and straightforward language, in the last decades of the Mughal Empire, its rulers were reduced to ignominious vassalage to foreign usurpers. Understandably, the Indo-Muslim elite were traumatised. The 'Islamicate' culture-power formation with which they identified profoundly was disintegrating and passing into history.

Ayesha Jalal writes that Muslims suffered from 'uprootedness and lack of direction' with the 'attenuation' of Mughal power.[108] North Indian Muslim society was so despondent at this juncture that it palpably reflected in the literature that it

---

106 Nicholas B. Dirks, *The Hollow Crown. Ethnohistory of an Indian Kingdom* (Cambridge, New York, New Rochelle, Melbourne, Sydney: CUP, 2008), p.384.

107 Ibid.

108 *Self and Sovereignty. Individual and Community in South Asia Islam Since 1850* (New Delhi: OUP, 2001), p.13.

produced. For instance, Jalal writes that a distinct type of Urdu poetry called *shahr-i-ashoob* or *ashoobiā shāiri* emerged in the 'late Mughal period'.[109] Literally 'lament for the city,' this poetic genre 'encapsulated' the 'socio-cultural turbulence' that cities in the Mughal realm were then undergoing.[110] It seems that Jalal is referring to the disruption of the 'moral economy' of the old Mughal urban centers discussed by Bayly. At the beginning of this chapter, we saw how, in the early nineteenth century, Mughal urban authorities like the *kotwāl* and the *kāzi* were losing credibility while the Hindu urban elite were getting increasingly assertive and powerful. The unravelling of long-standing power relations in which they were the dominant and Hindus the dominated must have been deeply unsettling for the *ashrāf* who produced and patronised Urdu poetry.

The 'Islamicate' cultural paradigm, once projected and undergirded by the Mughal Empire, was now seriously imperiled. The EIC administration just did not care for it. We have already seen Peter Hardy writing as much. Resultantly, in the words of Francis Robinson, 1820s and 1830s onwards, 'Perso-Islamic high culture dissolved with almost shocking speed'.[111] This was primarily due to, as he writes, 'the increasingly confident assertion of the new imperial power and culture of Britain in the administration of the land'.[112] For example, in 1835, the

109 Ibid., p.11.

110 Ibid.

111 'Perso-Islamic Culture in India from the Seventeenth to the Early Twentieth Century' in *The 'Ulama' of Farangi Mahall and Islamic Culture in South Asia* (Permanent Black, 2001), p.31

112 Ibid.

British replaced Persian with English as the official language of the state and that of the higher courts. Later, in 1837, regional languages were adopted in place of Persian in the lower courts.[113] With the legal administration discontinuing the use of Persian, a major avenue of employment that Persian learning once provided ceased to exist. Simultaneously, Persian poets and scholars were having a hard time as the Muslim gentry, a major source of support and patronage, were in decline due to political change, or the ascendence of 'monied men' and Hindu landholding communities. The *ulāmā* and Sufis, on the other hand, were 'more and more' taking to transmitting Islamic knowledge in the regional languages.[114] Persian was no more the language of cultural power *par excellence* as in the heydays of the Mughal Empire. Urdu, the second most preferred literary language by Indian Muslims, was faring no better in education and administration. Mushirul Hasan writes that the second half of the nineteenth century ushered an 'inglorious era in the history of the Urdu language'.[115] In Delhi, the one-time heart of the Mughal imperium, where Urdu had flowered and flourished, it was replaced by English as the language of administration and bureaucracy.[116] The 'Islamicate' cultural paradigm was ceasing to be hegemonic. This, as it seems,

113 Ibid., p.32.

114 Ibid., p.33.

115 'Sharif Culture and Colonial Rule: A *Maulvi*-Missionary Encounter' in *Living Together Separately*, p.334.

116 Ibid.

caused the *ashrāf* to become rather acutely aware of their loss of status. They now sought succour in 'their memory of the Perso-Islamic past'.[117] Since this was a past in which they had been rulers, *ashrāf* society, it seems, grew gradually obsessed with the idea of retrieving its power. Francis Robinson writes that the *ashrāf* thought that 'Power, and its management, was in their blood. It was their birthright'.[118] 'This feeling,' according to him, 'was at the heart of modern Muslim politics as they developed in northern India'.[119]

One comes across a situation, considered by David Gilmartin, wherein the colonial administration appears to be expressing its authority in an 'Islamicate' cultural paradigm. For example, the custodians of Sufi shrines in Punjab, known as *sajjādā nishins,* were actively courted by the British. They were selected to serve as local representatives in the rural administration of the province as '*zaildārs*, honorary magistrates, and district board members'.[120] However, it seems reasonable to argue that, they were, at the end of the day, mere subordinate agents of the colonial state. They did not render British authority 'Islamicate' in character by associating themselves with it. Prior to the British, the *sajjādā nishins* had

---

117 'Perso-Islamic Culture in India from the Seventeenth to the Early Twentieth Century' in *The 'Ulama' of Farangi Mahall and Islamic Culture in South Asia*, p.40.

118 Ibid.

119 Ibid.

120 *Empire and Islam. Punjab and the Making of Pakistan* (Delhi, Bombay, Calcutta, Madras: OUP, 1989), p.50. A *zail*, Gilmartin explains in the 'Glossary,' was an administrative subdivision in Punjab. The functionary in charge of it was called '*zaildar*' (p.237).

given their cooperation to the Mughals. Then, writes Gilmartin, they had served to 'dramatise the religious foundations' of the regime.[121] In other words, we might say that the *sajjādā nishins* used to reify the 'Islamicate' aura of Mughal rule. But the state that had replaced it sought to project no such aura, nor did the *sajjādā nishins* embody it. Based on what Gilmartin observes, one surmises that this matter was noticed by the *ulāmā* in Punjab. They thought that 'Structures of mediation could no longer effectively define a Muslim community's presence in colonial India'.[122] The *ulāmā* in Punjab now founded their actions on the idea that 'a fundamental reordering of Muslim life was required'.[123] They undertook a program of Islamic reform under which they attacked the religious authority and power of the *sajjādā nishins*.[124] The reformist *ulāmā* emphasised 'personal adherence to the basic duties of Islam' instead and undermined the 'conceptual system of rural Islam' in Punjab.[125] Simply put, the *ulāmā* were seeking to deprive the *sajjādā nishins* of legitimacy in the eyes of the believers as they were now the allies of a state which did not derive its moral discourse from Islam.

Did the colonial state, stepping into the political space left vacant by the retreat of Mughal sovereignty, possess

121 Ibid., p.45.
122 Ibid., p.56.
123 Ibid.
124 Ibid., p.55.
125 Ibid., p.56.

a cultural persona of its own? There is no doubt that many EIC officials were staunch Christians and very committed to 'spiritual change' in India.[126] They, in simple language, wanted Indians to give up their heathen ways and resort to the Christian truth. The most prominent among them was of course Charles Grant (1746-1823) who became the Chairman of the EIC in 1805. In this sense, a certain Christian evangelist intent undoubtedly underlay 'coloniality,' as J. Sai Deepak has recently demonstrated.[127] But this made the EIC state, at most, to borrow a phrase from C.A. Bayly, 'a covert confessional state'.[128] To term it a 'Christian realm' would definitely be a stretch. In terms of its symbols and ceremonials, the state that the EIC created in India was definitely not Christian, not even after the Charter Act of 1813 permitted missionaries to preach in its territories. In the aftermath of the uprising of 1857, even if there were still zealots in Westminster who wanted to see Indians being converted to Christianity, the British establishment adopted an avowed policy of leaving Indian customs and religions alone. The Queen's proclamation of 1858, thus, assured freedom of religion to all Indians. In actual practice, this amounted to a policy of, to borrow a phrase from Shashi Joshi and Bhagwan Josh, 'even handedness

---

126 'Returning the British to South Asian History: The Limits of Colonial Hegemony' in *Origins of Nationality in South Asia. Patriotism and Ethical Government in the Making of Modern India* (New Delhi: OUP, 2001), p.280.

127 See *India that is Bharat. Coloniality, Civilisation, Constitution* (New Delhi: Bloomsbury, 2021).

128 'Returning the British to South Asian History: The Limits of Colonial Hegemony' in *Origins of Nationality in South Asia*, p.280.

between communities'[129] which came to be defined primarily in the religious sense. This mainly religious understanding of the community that the British exhibited in India was the end outcome of their persistent efforts to classify and taxonomize Indians.

Throughout its existence, the colonial administration diligently gathered varieties of classificatory data about Indians. As observed by B.S. Cohn, there was an 'enumerative modality'[130] to the British efforts of arriving at the definition of the required 'body of information' and the procedures of gathering, ordering and classifying 'appropriate knowledge'.[131] Under this 'enumerative modality,' the British undertook censuses to count and categorise Indians by 'age, occupation, caste, religion, literacy, place of birth, and current residence'.[132] Thus, Cohn thinks that the colonial administration created the 'social categories by which India was ordered for administrative purposes'.[133] Nicholas B. Dirks, on the other hand, contends that, following the uprising of 1857, the British created in India an 'ethnographic state'. British 'imperial ambition, and anxiety'[134] were now focused on identifying the loyal and disloyal communities of Indians. As a result, according

129 *Struggle for Hegemony in India, Vol. 3, Culture Community and Power* (New Delhi: Sage Publications, 1994), p.36.

130 *Colonialism and Forms of Knowledge. The British in India* (Princeton, New Jersey: Princeton University Press, 1996), p.8.

131 Ibid., p.5.

132 Ibid., p.8.

133 Ibid.

134 *Castes of Mind. Colonialism and the Making of Modern India* (Delhi: Permanent Black, 2016 [Ninth Impression]), p.43.

to Dirks, 'anthropology supplanted history as the principal colonial modality of knowledge and rule'.[135] 1870 onwards, he claims, the colonial ethnographic curiosity especially flowered taking 'caste as the primary object of social classification and understanding'.[136] Based on what Cohn says, we may perhaps observe that the British approached Indian identities from various perspectives and apprehended various aspects to them. At a point, as Dirks argues, they might even have thought that 'caste' (or the 'jati') was the most dominant and relevant facet of the social identities of Indians. However, when it came to actually dealing with Indians, it seems that their religious identities eventually acquired an overriding salience in the eyes of the colonial administrators. This was definitely so by the end of the nineteenth century when, it seems, the British more and more understood Indians as a congeries of religious communities. This 'privileging of the religious factor in the definition of identity' by the colonial state, according to Ayesha Jalal, had 'the most decisive bearing on the projection of consciousness by individuals variously situated within the colonial system'.[137] When Indians approached the colonial system, it was as members or representatives of religious communities rather than as individuals.

As we see, the situation as it developed in colonial India in the second half of the nineteenth century was thus—On the one hand, the colonial state did not project a cultural

135 Ibid.

136 Ibid.

137 *Self and Sovereignty*, p.42.

persona. Unlike the Mughal Empire it did not undergird a particular cultural paradigm. On the other hand, it understood communities and identities primarily in the religious sense and was committed to treating them 'evenly'. As Gyanendra Pandey puts it, the colonial state was very 'self-consciously "neutral"—standing above society.'[138] At least for form's sake, thus, the colonial administration was meant to make a show of being 'fair' to all religious groups, without unduly favouring one. This opened a veritable Pandora's box. As subjects of the British Empire, Indians now approached the colonial administration as ostensible representatives of their religious communities and made demands upon it or sought the redress of perceived wrongs and grievances. We see that that is exactly what began to happen on a large scale in the second half of the nineteenth century. The colonial state was faced by large scale group actions which sought to promote, defend, or secure greater visibility for, this or that cultural symbol or ceremonial in the public sphere. In large tracts of North India, Hindu groups forcefully challenged the erstwhile symbols of 'Islamicate' hegemony, namely the Urdu language and the customary Muslim practice of sacrificing cows on Eid al-Adha, or Bakr-Id. They promoted Hindi written in the Devanagari script and mobilised to defend the cow. Finally, they sought to make the public observance of Hindu festivals more spectacular. In conventional academia, these phenomena have been given the blanket designation of

138 *The Construction of Communalism in Colonial North India* (New Delhi: OUP, Oxford India Perennials, 2012 [Third Edition]), p.16.

'communalism'. This term is, unfortunately, misleading and does not capture the essence of what was actually happening. Increasingly, Hindus were deploying their cultural symbols and public ceremonials to push back against the 'Islamicate' cultural symbols and their hegemony. Colonial North India was entering a phase of intense cultural contests and conflicts.

According to Gyanendra Pandey, 'the issue of cow-protection' 'sparked off a new level of public debate' and was pushed into 'limelight' in eastern UP in 1887-88. This happened as the Allahabad High Court refused to give protection to the cow 'as an object of religious worship'.[139] A few years later, around the Bakr-Id of 1893, 'a large-scale attack was mounted' upon Muslims by Hindus in the weaving town of Azamgarh.[140] The objective of the attackers was of course keeping them from ritually slaughtering cows to observe Bakr-Id. Pandey thinks that the cow-protection movement became more 'aggressive' as the 1880s gave way to the 90s and its geographical base shifted from Punjab and Central Provinces to eastern UP and Bihar.[141] He links the rising bellicosity of the movement to the social dynamics of the region. Apparently, the wealthy and the highly-placed who had hitherto patronised the cow-protection societies, or Gaurakshini Sabhas, were now taking a 'back seat'.[142] In other words, those enjoying the most

139 Ibid., p.163.
140 Ibid., p.164.
141 Ibid., p.175.
142 Ibid., p.176.

conspicuous social prestige no more provided leadership to the cow-protection agitation. Instead, as observed by Pandey, its leadership was now passing into the hands of, if we might use the term, the 'lesser elite'. Cow-protection agitation, we are told, was being taking over by people whom colonial officials described as 'half-educated English-speaking agitators,'[143] namely, 'small zamindars, professionals and traders with little direct bureaucratic connections'.[144] They were assisted by a 'motley crew of swamis, sanyasis and fakirs'.[145]

The aforementioned protagonists of the cow adopted tropes that would resonate with all Hindus. They termed the cow the 'universal mother,' as human beings are nourished by her milk, and home to the Deities. Alongside, they posited Muslims, the English, and Indian Christians as 'the killers of the cow and, hence, the…[enemies] of Hinduism'.[146] The new vanguard of the cow-protection agitation did not just stop at rhetoric and imagery as it tried to mobilise large-scale support in favour of its efforts, it resorted to more concrete means and measures too. For instance, *sabhās*, or meetings, were conducted to exhort Hindus to undertake cow-protection. Publicity was generated and masses were mobilised for these events through 'circular letters'.[147] Called *patiās*, these letters listed the 'extreme consequences' that would befall those who

143 Ibid.
144 Ibid., pp.176-177.
145 Ibid., p.177.
146 Ibid., p.179.
147 Ibid., p.181.

failed to respond to the 'appeals for action and propaganda contained in them'.[148] The cow-protection agitators did not even spare 'threats of excommunication'[149] as they sought to rally Hindus in the aid of the cow. A standard fund-raising technique adopted by them appears to have been the collection of *chutkī*, or household contribution of grain. It was later converted to cash (presumably through sale). This task was assigned to a local agent, called *sabhāsad*, in every village and urban neighborhood, or *muhallā*.[150] The broad outcome of the cow-protection agitation, it seems, was a generally greater level of cohesion and assertiveness among Hindus. As Sandria Freitag puts it, 'The organisational structure created to espouse and protect an ideology centered on the cow related to the general process by which articulation of Hindu community sharpened'.[151]

Why were the 'lesser elite,' as we termed them, stepping up to take charge of the cow-protection agitation? One surmises that some of them were in a rather embattled state at this historical juncture. For instance, according to Freitag, Bumihars and Rajputs, the two prominent landowning *jātis* of eastern UP, had suffered 'land losses' which had been 'picked up by Ahirs'.[152] Thus, it appears that they were in urgent need of a cause that would boost their declining social prestige. Cow-

148 Ibid., p.184.

149 Ibid., p.185.

150 Sandria B. Freitag, *Collective Action and Community. Public Arenas and Emergence of Communalism in North India* (New Delhi: OUP, 1990), p.153.

151 Ibid., p.156.

152 Ibid., p.166.

protection was just that cause. Reassertion of declining status might have been the motivation why Rajputs and Bhumihars (along with Brahman landowners) 'provided a large part of the fighting force' that attacked the Bakr-Id celebrations in Azamgrah in the year 1893.[153]

The declining elite were joined by ascendent groups who were taking up cow-protection to project a newly acquired social status. Freitag writes that the peasants who were 'higher in status and holdings' were 'growing wealthier' as they 'profited by fixed rates and favorable tenures'.[154] According to her, they 'proved willing and able to support cow related values' being 'in the process of securing legitimacy for their claims to higher social status'.[155] Pandey too points out how 'less privileged communities were organising their own autonomous [cow-protection] movements at this time'.[156] He notices increasing activity in cow-protection by *jātis* like the Kurmis, Koeris, and Ahirs.[157] As they were largely engaged in peasant production, it is very possible (based on what Freitag writes) that segments of these social groups were economically doing better and tried to publicise their social ascendence by organising cow-protection. Especially the Ahirs (now known by the caste name 'Yadav') who, we have been told, had gained in landownership, and were 'very prominent' in the cow-protection riots.[158] The *jātis* who

153 *The Construction of Communalism in Colonial North India*, p.188.

154 *Collective Action and Community*, p.166.

155 Ibid.

156 *The Construction of Communalism in Colonial North India*, p.192.

157 Ibid., pp.192-193.

158 Ibid., p.193.

traditionally sought their means in trades or the professions also participated in the cow-protection agitation. Pandey notes that the Kayasths and Banias, though stretched 'fairly thin on the ground,' were among the cow-protection activists.[159] Cow-protection, thus, involved a very significant cross section of the Hindu society of the (as we term it today) Hindi heartland and articulated its anxieties and aspirations. It was probably, in this sense, something very akin to a 'popular movement'.

The Hindi-Nagari movement was an exact contemporary of the cow-protection efforts in the Hindi belt, and it seemingly gained a comparable social traction in terms of the numbers it mobilised. Its popularity could be because it judiciously combined the pursuit of a worldly agenda with genuine idealism. According to Christopher R. King, the Hindi-Nagari movement 'represented increasing numbers of educated Hindus' who viewed Hindi 'not only as a potential means to government service, but also as a vehicle of cultural and religious values'.[160] The objective of the Hindi-Nagari movement was to replace Urdu with Hindi written in the Devanagari script as the official language of the North-Western Provinces and Oudh (as Uttar Pradesh was called in the nineteenth century). It is hard to pinpoint the exact historical moment when this movement began. However, it is evident, as observed by King, that debates and controversies between the champions of Urdu and Hindi had begun in the 1860s. For instance, he alludes to Garcin de

159 Ibid.

160 *One Language Two Scripts. The Hindi Movement in Nineteenth Century North India* (Bombay: OUP, 1994), p.118.

Tassy, a French scholar of languages, reporting in 1866 that 'a great dispute had arisen between Hindus and Muslims over the respective merits of Hindi and Urdu…'[161] It was not long after that the 'great dispute' was playing out in the form of petitions, memorials, and memorandums to the government as well as journalistic activism. Babu Shiva Prasad (1823-1895), identified by King as 'a prominent official of the provincial Department of Public Instruction,' composed a memorandum advocating Hindi as the official language of the province in 1868.[162] Again, in 1869, the 'Hindi-Urdu controversy occupied more space in the Hindi and Urdu newspapers of the NWP than any other single subject'.[163] In 1873, the advocates of Hindi presented a memorial to the Lieutenant-Governor of the province, Sir William Muir (1819-1905), making very detailed arguments against the continued use of Urdu for official purposes. The memorialists thought that 'the Persian (Urdu) script made court documents illegible, encouraged forgery, facilitated the use of incomprehensible Arabic and Persian words, and had a foreign origin…'[164] Further, they contended that 'the bulk of the population used Hindi and only a part of the higher classes…had become used to Persian…'[165] In other words, they were forcing the point that Hindi was the language of the Hindus who were in a majority and ought to

161 Ibid., p.128.
162 Ibid., p.130.
163 Ibid., p.129.
164 Ibid., p.131.
165 Ibid.

be favoured by the government. About a decade later, in 1882, when notables of the province gave evidence before the Indian Education Commission headed by W.W. Hunter, the religious identification of Hindi and Urdu was complete. As Francis Robinson puts it pithily, 'The Muslims supported Urdu, the Hindus, Hindi'.[166]

Along with petitions, memorials, memorandums, and controversies prosecuted in the newspapers, a case for Hindi was made through drama and poetry. King writes that the dominant theme they presented was that of 'the virtue and morality of Nagari or Hindi with the vice and immorality of Urdu…'[167] One of the examples he cites of this literature is a four-hundred stanza poem titled *Hindī Urdū kī Larāi* by one Sohan Prasad. It was published in 1885. We see that Prasad anthropomorphised Hindi and Urdu as two quarrelling women and got the former to utter copious invectives against the latter. In Prasad's poem, Hindi calls Urdu 'a prostitute,' 'a murderer,' 'unclean,' and '*mlecch*'. She threatens to seize Urdu 'by the hair, throw her down, and pull out her teeth'[168] Prasad underlines, we feel, the spiritual kinship of the Hindi-Nagari and cow-protection agitations when he has Hindi bring up cow slaughter.[169] He castigates Hindus for being idle as cows are butchered by the *mlecch*.[170]

166 *Separatism among Indian Muslims*, p.76.
167 *One Language Two Scripts*, p.137.
168 Ibid., p.138.
169 Ibid.
170 Ibid., p.139.

The most prominent organisational face of the Hindi-Nagari movement was the Nagari Pracharini Sabha (NPS). Founded in 1893, it provided, as King puts it 'a body of men emotionally and intellectually devoted to the growth of their chosen language and script…'[171] What were their social backgrounds? We learn that Brahmans made up over 40 per cent of the membership. The remaining members came from the Bhumihar, Rajput, Agarwal, and Vaishya *jātis*.[172] Once again, the demographics of the NPS seem to testify to the very respectable social traction of the Hindi-Nagari agitation that we alluded to above; the Sabha appears to have represented, if we might say, an alliance of the higher and middle-ranked *jātis*. The NPS undertook wide ranging initiatives to promote the cause of Hindi. It, to give a few examples, searched for old Hindi manuscripts, established a library, and published Hindi works and a Hindi journal.[173] In the summer of 1896, the NPS began a province-wide campaign for Hindi-Nagari. It created a special sub-committee and sent representatives to nineteen districts of the province, most of them eastern ones. Eventually, sixty-thousand signatures were gathered and appended to a memorial that delicately urged the government to implement Nagari usage in legal administration. Without demanding that the Urdu script be given up, the memorial requested that 'the written character of the immense majority of the people should

171 Ibid., p.127.
172 Ibid., p.144.
173 Ibid., p.127.

be used in government courts, and all summons, decisions and decrees should be issued in that character'.[174]

While the NPS was advancing the cause of Hindi-Nagari with great energy and dedication, Madan Mohan Malaviya (1861-1946) authored a book titled *Court Character and Primary Education in the N.-W.P. and Oudh*. Some of the arguments he made therein were that Hindi had been the medium of 'public business' in North India much before the Muslim invasions, that the majority of the population understood Hindi and not Urdu, and that the introduction of the Nagari script in courts and offices would 'lead to a simpler style'[175] akin to the language used by the people. By the end of the nineteenth century, newspapers were rife with the 'Hindi-Urdu controversy'. In 1899, we are told, articles and letters on the issue of Hindi versus Urdu were flooding the newspaper columns.[176] Maybe, this made the provincial administration sit up and take notice. Beginning in July 1899, the then Lieutenant-Governor Sir Antony MacDonnell (1844-1925) 'consulted with the provincial Board of Revenue, the High Court of the North-Western Provinces, and the Judicial Commissioner of Oudh'.[177] Finally, in April 1900, he issued a resolution which gave 'the Nagari script equal status with the Urdu [script] in certain areas of official business'.[178] It might

174 Ibid., p.149.
175 Ibid., p.151.
176 Ibid., p.152.
177 Ibid., p.153.
178 Ibid., p.126.

have been 'a largely symbolic victory' for the 'adherents' of Hindi-Nagari. [179] But in the charged atmosphere of the times, symbols mattered.

The Hindi-Nagari 'adherents' did not care for the argument, brought so often against them, that Urdu was the symbol of the 'syncretic culture' of the province, that is, it belonged equally to Hindus and Muslims. For instance, Syed Ahmed Khan thought that Urdu 'had been made by the common intercourse of all classes and communities' and warned of dire outcomes if 'the claims of Hindi/Nagari were pressed against it'.[180] However, it is obvious from the zeal of the champions of Hindi-Nagari that they took a very different view of reality. They did not see Urdu as a manifestation of cultural 'syncretism' but, as we would term it, an instrument of 'Islamicate' hegemony. Alok Rai seems to grasp this when he writes that *'this "syncretic" culture was merely the form in which traditional dominance was mediated to them'*[181] (italics in original). He acknowledges that the 'emergent Nagari/Hindi proto-elite simply *had* to challenge' this form of 'traditional dominance,' and in the 'historical circumstances' that existed 'the democratic popularity of the challenge was practically guaranteed'.[182] Simply put, it seems very plausible that those taking up Hindi-Nagari advocacy were expressing a popular aspiration of doing away with the cultural instruments

179 Ibid.

180 Alok Rai, *Hindi Nationalism* (Hyderabad: Orient BlackSwan, 2001 [Reprinted 2002, 2007, 2018]), p.60.

181 Ibid.

182 Ibid.

and symbols of Islamicate hegemony, now that a 'new political dispensation' was in place and 'Muslim colonialism was a thing of the past'.[183] After all, in the previous chapter, we saw how Urdu was intimately linked to the history of the Mughal Empire as an aspect of the culture-power formation that it was. And no, unlike what is claimed by King and Rai,[184] Hindi was not a colonial period fabrication by the pundits at the College of Fort William and Christian missionaries. Its roots were undeniably located in the antiquity that predated the Muslim invasions of India. Amrit Rai considers Apabhraṅśa, a language that extended its sway over North India ninth century onwards, 'the immediate precursor of Hindi'.[185] As about the Hindi language proper, he thinks that it began to develop in the eleventh century 'with Gorakhnath and the other Nath-Panthis'.[186] Examining pieces 'from the writings of Gorakhnath,' he concludes that 'his language is a form of Hindi/Hindavi...'[187] Amrit Rai is emphatic in dismissing the claim that the Hindi-Urdu split was initiated at the Fort William College. The split, according to him, 'was already a *fait accompli* when the British arrived upon the scene...'[188] This of course makes full sense when we remember how, in the

183 *Self and Sovereignty*, p.126.

184 See Chapter II, 'The Development of Differentiation' in *One Language, Two Scripts* and Chapter 3, 'The MacDonnell Moment' in *Hindi Nationalism*.

185 *A House Divided. The Origin and Development of Hindi/Hindavi* (Delhi: OUP, 1984), p.58.

186 Ibid., p.83.

187 Ibid., p.94.

188 Ibid., p.17.

eighteenth century, Urdu was systematically divested of Sanskrit words. The votaries of Hindi-Nagari were thus very correct in viewing Hindi and Urdu as articulations of two distinct cultural paradigms. And they were also right in regarding Hindi, in view of its Apabhraṅśa and Nath *sampradāya* parentage, their 'own' heritage. Certain prominent Indo-Muslim elites, it seems, nurtured a similar sentiment with regard to Urdu. For instance, Maulvi Mohammad Zakaullah (1832-1910), author of a fourteen-volume history of India in Urdu (*Tārikh-é-Hindustān*), thought that the 'religious and cultural mores of Muslims' were 'inextricably linked' to the language's future. He, writes Mushirul Hasan, 'clung tenaciously to Urdu, and resisted to the last the temptation to abandon it for English'.[189]

Hindu assertion and solidarity were not restricted to organising cow-protection and promoting the official usage of Hindi-Nagari. Increasingly, in the second half of the nineteenth century, we come across instances of Hindus attempting to observe their festivals with a defiant splendour and verve in the urban spaces of North India. Such 'public arena activities,' as Sandria Freitag terms them, further fostered a sense of cohesion among Hindus overriding the specific and the local, or 'localized perceptions of community'. Borrowing an expression from

189 Mushirul Hasan, *A Moral Reckoning. Muslim Intellectuals in Nineteenth Century Delhi* (New Delhi: OUP, 2005), p.211.

the cultural anthropologist Victor Turner, Freitag calls this heightened sense of community 'communitas'.[190] What is it about festivals that they generated communitas among Hindus? When involving a procession, they could be an 'important experience and statement of group solidarity,' or 'a kind of metaphor for the process of group identification'.[191] Giving rise to 'enthusiasm and shouting,' such occasions fused 'discrete elements…into an interlinking whole'.[192] Further, these 'public ceremonials' worked 'to exclude those considered outsiders'.[193] They, apparently, evoked the 'definition of community' which 'stressed shared characteristics and values and drew boundaries that were simultaneously inclusive and exclusive'.[194]

Hindu communitas must have been a major cultural challenge faced by the Indo-Muslim elite who had once dominated the *qasbās* and lent them an Islamicate character. We draw this inference from the instance of Bareilly where 'new Hindu merchant and Brahmin arrivals pushed for expanded recognition of their religious values and ceremonials…'[195] This indicated that the old elite were no more in charge in this very important *qasbā* and the former balance of 'urban power' had 'shifted'.[196] The Hindus of Bareilly, thus, became unwilling to restrict or limit the public observance of their

190 *Collective Action and Community*, p.91.
191 Ibid., p.131.
192 Ibid., p.134.
193 Ibid., p.138.
194 Ibid.
195 Ibid., p.108.
196 Ibid.

sacred ceremonials. In 1870, they announced that 'they would take out the *Rāmnaumī* [procession] during Muharram'.[197] Forcing a compromise, the colonial administration intervened and divided the day between the Ram Navami and Muharram processions. The arrangement, however, did not satisfy the newly assertive Bareilly Hindus. Apparently, they were not ready to settle for anything less than the right to take out a religious procession at the same time as the Muslims. In protest, Freitag informs, the Hindus of Bareilly 'refused to hold their procession' and 'closed their shops for four days'.[198] We infer that this was an occasion when the Bareilly Hindus expressed, 'in symbolic and ideological terms,' the 'sense of a larger community' within 'the structures of urban life'.[199] They were going beyond the 'relational "community" to the broader one'.[200] In the process, the strong *jāti* sentiments which had earlier kept apart the Baniyas and Brahmans, the Kayasths and Khatris in this urban context were frequently overcome.[201] Hindu communitas, as it seems, was becoming a socially palpable phenomenon and a solvent for the Islamicate cultural persona of the *qasbās*. Driven by a newly acquired, ideologically formulated trans-local solidarity (which communitas apparently was), Hindus were undertaking aggressive group action to rewrite the cultural script of the North Indian urban spaces—they were

197 Ibid., p.109.
198 Ibid.
199 Ibid., p.125.
200 Ibid.
201 Ibid.

increasingly enforcing the dominance of their own cultural symbols and ceremonials therein. The result was a general deterioration of Hindu-Muslim relations across colonial North India in the 1880s and 90s.

The ongoing cultural conflicts were further exacerbated by the introduction of local self-government, or the democratic principle in the administration of urban spaces. Municipal boards with a majority of elective seats were created in 1883.[202] As it turned out immediately, outnumbered by Hindus, Muslims found themselves generally disadvantaged in municipal politics and elections. Further, as Hindus dominated and controlled the local bodies, they began using them to push their own cultural agendas. As Francis Robinson writes, Hindus 'could defend the cow and impose their standards on Muslims' through the putative promotion of the 'hygienic management of slaughter houses and kebab shops'.[203] In such a situation, maintaining the right to slaughter and eat cows would become a matter of protecting their religion and culture for the Muslims.[204] Local bodies, as a result, became yet another site for the ongoing cultural conflicts. In brief, it is plausible to suppose that the experience of local self-government made Indian Muslims

---

202 C.A. Bayly, 'Local Control in Indian Towns – The Case of Allahabad. 1880-1920' in *Modern Asian Studies.* Vol. 5, No. 4 (1971), pp.289-311. P.309.

203 'Municipal Government and Muslim Separatism in the United Provinces. 1883 to 1916' in *Modern Asian Studies.* Vol. 7, No. 3 (1973), pp.389-441. P.393.

204 Ibid.

wary of ballot based representative politics.

According to Francis Robinson, the franchise (at the local level) 'gave a marked advantage' to Hindu money lenders and traders. He terms them 'new men'.[205] This could be because, as we gather, they had been gaining in means and social prestige for a while. After 1857, for example, 'money-lenders pursued property with vigor'[206] while the majority of those losing land were Muslims and Rajputs.[207] Hindu traders and money-lenders, it appears, were chiefly instrumental in the marginalisation of Muslims in the local bodies. Robinson writes that 'Where traders were active, dispossessed Muslims found it difficult to find any representation at all'.[208] Along with money-lenders, traders were 'most vigorous in the assertion of Hindu religion and values'.[209] For instance, in Allahabad, they allied with 'professional men' during the 1880s to transfer control of the Magh Mela 'from the Muslim Kotwal to the Hindu subcommittee of the municipal board'. They succeeded in this objective in 1886.[210] No doubt, in 1888, a Muslim organization by the name of Anjuman-i-Rifah-i-Islam demanded the abolition of the existing municipal board in the city and fixing the number of Hindu and Muslim seats to

205 Ibid., p.396.
206 Ibid., p.401.
207 Ibid., p.405.
208 Ibid., p.408.
209 Ibid.
210 Ibid., p.410.

ensure representation for Muslims.[211]

By the turn of the twentieth century, as the newspaper reports cited by Robinson indicate, cultural agendas and conflicts were being aggressively prosecuted through local politics. After they gained the electoral 'upper hand' in Moradabad, Hindus forced Muslim butchers to dry their hides outside the city.[212] Then in Bijnor, where the board was dominated by Hindus, Muslim butchers were thrashed by the Hindu kotwal for selling beef.[213] Muslims retaliated when they could. Cows were openly killed in Najibabad after the Muslims won power.[214] However, one assumes that Muslims did not get to even the score that often as they were steadily yielding to Hindus in local politics. Between 1884 and 1908, we are told, Muslims 'steadily' lost seats in some very important cities and towns of the United Provinces such as Meerut, Agra, Kanpur, Moradabad, Badaun, and Chandpur.[215]

Local politics in neighboring Punjab were a mirror image of UP's. As we see in the 1880s, the 'urban classes' there made local elections a 'test of communal strength'.[216] Apparently, a method that Hindus often chose was putting economic pressure on indebted Muslims—moneylenders would make their Muslim clients vote for their favored Hindu candidates.

211 Ibid.

212 Ibid., p.413.

213 Ibid.

214 Ibid.

215 *Separatism among Indian Muslims*, p.82.

216 N. Gerald Barrier, 'The Punjab Government and Communal Politics,' *The Journal of Asian Studies*, Vol. 27, No. 3 (May, 1968), pp.523-539. P. 536.

Sikhs generally took the side of Hindus. In many smaller municipalities the rich went to the extent of hiring thugs who guarded voting booths and stopped their enemies from casting their votes. There were even cases of candidates stealing ballot boxes before counting. Fake registrations and ballot papers were resorted to commonly.[217] According to Gerald Barrier, Hindus won the majority of the local elections 'because they composed the large middle-class population in the central and eastern towns'.[218] With their superior education, they handled electioneering better. Barrier provides us data from 1883 and 84 which shows that Hindus won a majority on seventy-two committees in ninety-six reported elections.[219] It was against this backdrop of the overwhelming Hindu dominance of local politics, that the Indian National Congress came by and demanded representative bodies for British India at large.

---

217 Ibid., p.536.

218 Ibid.

219 Ibid.

1885-1906 MONSTROUS AND UNREASONABLE SCHEMES
THE ANXIOUS INDO-MUSLIM ELITE

A CRUCIAL HISTORICAL TURN

AS WE SAW, the nineteenth century was a challenging time for the Indo-Muslim elite. They suffered a relative reduction of their means and witnessed the Islamicate cultural paradigm they represented gradually attenuating. The colonial administration treated the cultural tropes of *ashrāf* life with scant regard, while Hindus got increasingly assertive with their cultural symbols. On since the start of the nineteenth century, when Mughal administration was losing its efficacy, Hindu cultural assertion got especially forceful with the introduction of local self-government. Due to their advantage in numbers, Hindus dominated the local bodies and frequently used them to implement their cultural agendas. Meanwhile, the Indo-Muslim elite had engineered a more socially and culturally coherent Indian Muslim society through 'reform' efforts. As we suggested, they, in the process, seem to have arrogated to themselves a more conspicuous leadership role in it (while Indian Muslim society might have looked up to them anyway). Then, the Indo-Muslim elite sought to cope by configuring their own versions of modernity and a *modus vivendi* with British rule. The institutions at Deoband and Aligarh expressed this quest. The latter, especially, as we saw, was a much more ambitious project which aimed at a thorough regeneration of Indian Muslim society. At this crucial historical turn, ten years after the founding of the Muhammadan Anglo-Oriental College at Aligarh, an all-India political organisation came into existence. It offered a vision of political nationhood for India. And it made the Indo-Muslim elite very anxious by demanding that the colonial state implement, what were for the times, some rather radical political reforms.

'BUILDING BONDS' AND 'MENDING CLEAVAGES' – AN IMAGINATION OF NATIONHOOD

On 28 December 1885, seventy-two delegates gathered 'timidly and unobtrusibly'[1] at an unassuming venue in Bombay to form the Indian National Congress (hereafter only Congress). Proclaimed from the auditorium of Gokuldas Tejpal Sanskrit College, the Congress was unprecedented in both scope and ambition. The organisations that had preceded it were

1 Homy Mody, *Sir Pherozeshah Mehta: A Political Biography* (Delhi: Asia Publishing House, 1963), p. 100.

either strictly provincial or class centric in character.[2] Only Surendranath Bannerjee's Indian Association, established in 1876, had seemingly attempted to be an exception to the rule.[3] The Congress, thus, despite its modest inception, articulated a much bolder vision, we are told that it was one of 'creating a community or nation of all Indians'.[4] Apparently, this vision was in the works for some time. As John R. McLane observes, western educated Indians had been forming 'local political associations in the major cities beginning in the middle of the century'. The establishment of the Congress was but a continuation of these 'local efforts to influence government policy'. Besides, the formation of local level political bodies and then the Congress, according to McLane, was an exercise

2 The earlier organizations were not of a pronouncedly political nature and promoted the interests of the colonial landed elite. For example, the Landholders' Society, founded in 1837, was an association of the landholders of Bengal, Bihar and Odisha. The Bengal British India Society, formed in 1843, was similarly an organization of the Bengal landlords. In 1851, it merged with the Landholders' Society and became the British Indian Association. There were similar bodies in other Presidencies, like the Bombay Association and the Madras Native Association (both established in 1852). Both were dominated by the landed gentry. Other, smaller, organizations like the Poona Sarvajanik Sabha (1867) and the Madras Mahajana Sabha (1884) were of a similar nature.

3 Its 'national' aspirations showed in the fact that, besides Calcutta, the Indian Association had branches in Kanpur, Allahabad, and Lahore. But, as S.R. Mehrotra tells us, these were controlled mostly by expatriate Bengalis, while the organization at large was 'dominated by a few young and ambitious men with advanced views on the political and social questions of the day.' [See S.R Mehrotra, *A History of the Indian National Congress, Vol. I, 1885-1918* (Delhi: Vikas Publishing House, 1995), p. 3.]

4 John R. McLane, *Indian Nationalism and the Early Congress,* (Princeton University Press, 1977), p. 3.

in 'building bonds between members of traditional ethnic groups where they were absent, and mending cleavages when new ones appeared'.[5] Thus, one might say that the Congress was the natural, all-India level, outcome of a range of civil society initiatives by Indians wherein individuals were 'bound together by choice and the perception of shared interests rather than ascribed status'.[6]

It appears that the Congress took the task of 'building bonds' and 'mending cleavages' quite seriously. As put by W.C. Bonnerji (1844-1906), the first President of the Congress, its objectives were, among other things, the 'promotion of personal intimacy and friendship' between those who seek to work for the country and abolition of 'all possible race, creed, or provincial prejudices'.[7] Dr Rajendralal Mitra (1822-1891) echoed Bonnerji the next year when he addressed the Congress as the Chairman of its Reception Committee. He forcefully reaffirmed that the Congress is committed to creating an Indian nation. Dr Mitra declared that he wanted the 'scattered units' of 'his race' to 'coalesce and come together' so that they may 'live as a nation'.[8] He saw in the Congress the 'commencement

---

5 Ibid.

6 Judith M. Brown, *Modern India. The Origins of an Asian Democracy* (OUP, 1994), p.172.

7 A.M. Zaidi and S. Zaidi, eds., *The Encyclopedia of the Indian National Congress, Vol. I, 1885-1900, The Founding Fathers* (New Delhi: S. Chand & Company Ltd., 1976), p. 46.

8 Indian National Congress Proceedings, Microfilm No. 1433, *Detailed Report of the Proceedings of the Second Indian National Congress Held at Calcutta on the 27th, 28th, 29th and 30th of December, 1886* (New Delhi: National Archives of India), p.47.

of such a coalescence'.[9] In 1890, the President-elect of the year Pherozeshah Mehta (1845-1915) yet again asserted that the 'members of the Congress meet together as men on the common basis of nationality…'[10]

The 'common basis of nationality' that had supposedly engendered the Congress was most eloquently expounded in 1891 by P. Ananda Charlu (1843-1908), the President-elect of the year. He, during his address, berated the opponents of the Congress. Their intention, Charlu believed, was 'to detract from the worth and significance of the well-knit, ever-expanding phalanx known as the National Congress'.[11] They were doing this disingenuously, he believed, by contriving a 'desultory controversy'[12] on what makes a nation. Sometimes they proposed that 'a common religion' is the 'differentia' of a nation along with 'a common language; proved or provable common extraction'.[13] Some of these controversialists also added to the list 'the presence of the privileges of commensality and inter-conjugal kinship'.[14] For a mass of people to be regarded

9 Ibid.

10 Indian National Congress Proceedings, Microfilm No. 1433, *Detailed Report of the Proceedings of the Sixth Indian National Congress Held at Calcutta on the 26th, 27th, 29th and 30th of December, 1890* (New Delhi: National Archives of India), p.6.

11 Indian National Congress Proceedings, Microfilm No. 1433, *Detailed Report of the Proceedings of the Seventh Indian National Congress Held at Nagpur on the 28th, 29th and 30th of December, 1891* (New Delhi: National Archives of India), p.6.

12 Ibid.

13 Ibid.

14 Ibid.

as a nation, they suggested, they must dine together and intermarry. Charlu dismissed these arguments emphatically. For Charlu, a nation was nothing but,

> the aggregate of those that are (to adopt and adapt the words of a writer in the *National Review*)—Citizens of one country, subordinate to one power, subject to one supreme legislature, taxed by one authority, influenced, for weal or woe, by one system of administration, urged by like impulses to secure like rights and to be relieved of like burdens.[15]

The Congress's conception of nationhood was, one can suggest in the light of the remarks made by Charlu, purely 'civic'. It was not language or a common (presumably racial) extraction that made a nation but subordination to the same political dispensation, taxation regime, administration, and one 'supreme legislature'. But a certain contradiction inhered in this imagination of the nation and rendered it vulnerable. This is revealed by the Congress's stand on the issue of social reform.

In 1886, Dadabhai Naoroji (1825-1917) had expressed impatience with those demanding that the Congress take up social reform. Speaking as its second President, Naoroji clarified that the Congress is a political body seeking to

15 Ibid.

represent 'political aspirations'.[16] Blaming the Congress for not discussing social reform, he argued, was like blaming 'the House of Commons for not discussing the abstruser (sic.) problems on mathematics or metaphysics'.[17] Besides, as he saw, there was another impediment to the Congress taking up social reform. Naoroji pointed out that in the Congress are 'Hindus of every caste, amongst whom, even in the same province, customs and social arrangements differs (sic.) widely are Mohammedans and Christians of various denominations, Parsis, Sikhs, Brahmos and what not…'[18] 'How can this gathering,' he asked the audience,

> 'of all classes discuss the social reforms needed in each individual class? …Only the members of that class can effectively deal with the reforms therein needed. A national Congress must confine itself to questions in which the entire nation has a direct participation…'[19]

The same sentiments were reiterated at the next annual Congress by Badruddin Tyabji (1844-1906), the President elect. Tyabji urged those who wanted the Congress to venture into social reform to see that it is composed of 'the representatives

16 Indian National Congress Proceedings, Microfilm No. 1433, *Detailed Report of the Proceedings of the Second Indian National Congress Held at Calcutta on the 27th. 28th, 29th and 30th of December, 1886* (New Delhi: National Archives of India), p.54.

17 Ibid.

18 Ibid.

19 Ibid.

of, not of any class or community, not of one part of India, but of all the different parts, and of all the different classes, and of all the different communities of India'.[20] Since each of these different communities had 'social problems' unique to them, Tyabji averred that their removal is 'best dealt with by the leaders of the particular community…' He, thus, thought that the,

> only wise and, indeed, the only possible course [the Congress] can adopt is to confine [its] discussions to such questions that affect the whole of India at large, and to abstain from the discussion of questions that affect a particular part or a particular community only.[21]

In 1892, W. C. Bonnerji too sought to clarify why the Congress must keep from meddling in social reform. He was rather brusquer than Tyabji in this. Re-elected the Congress President, he confessed that he is 'one of those who have very little faith in the public discussion of social matters'.[22] This was because, for him, social reform was something that 'ought to be left to the individuals of a community who belong to the same

---

20 Indian National Congress Proceedings, Microfilm No. 1433, *Detailed Report of the Proceedings of the Third Indian National Congress Held at Madras on the 27th, 28th, 29th and 30th of December, 1887* (New Delhi: National Archives of India), p.75.

21 Ibid.

22 Indian National Congress Proceedings, Microfilm No. 1433, *Detailed Report of the Proceedings of the Eighth Indian National Congress Held at Allahabad on the 28th, 29th and 30th of December, 1892* (New Delhi: National Archives of India), p.12.

social organisation'.[23] It could not be otherwise since, Bonnerji pointed out to the audience,

> How is it possible for a Hindu gentleman to discuss with a Parsi or a Mohamedan gentleman matters connected with Hindu social questions? How is it possible for a Mohamedan gentleman to discuss with Hindu or Parsi gentlemen matters connected with Mohamedan social questions? And how is it possible for a Parsi gentleman to discuss with Hindu and Mohamedan gentlemen matters connected with Parsi social customs?[24]

The contradiction that lay at the core of the Congress's conception of Indian nationhood was thus this—though it had been imagined in purely 'civic' terms, it was not constituted by individuals but by religious and normative groups. Interestingly, one notices that the Congress understood India somewhat in the same way as the colonial administration. Further, the Congress granted the constituent units of the Indian nation that it was imagining something akin to an 'internal sovereignty'. Their inner spaces, in terms of customs, mores, and values, were sacrosanct and not meant to be breached. Apparently, as the Congress saw it, there was to be no better way of ensuring this than following a strictly hands-off policy towards social reform and keeping to 'issues of a high level of general concern…'[25] As

23 Ibid.

24 Ibid.

25 *Modern India. The Origins of an Asian Democracy*, p.188.

a result, political reform was assigned 'to the national arena for public discussion and recommendation, and social reform to the local arena for private action.'[26]

'THESE MONSTROUS AND UNREASONABLE SCHEMES'

Due to the incongruity inherent in it, the Indian nation of Congress's conception was somewhat vulnerable. Its legitimacy could be easily challenged if sufficient numbers of the representatives of one of its religious or normative constituents did not join the Congress, its 'embodiment'. Or individuals could refuse to be counted in this nation as representatives of religious or normative groups.

As it turned out, the nation that the Congress was trying to forge had soon a missing bit pointed out. It was quickly noticed that the Congress is failing to draw the adherents of a certain religion in sufficient numbers. Commenting on the relatively inconspicuous attendance of Muslims at the first Congress, the Bombay correspondent of the *Times* newspaper said that 'they remained steadfast in their habitual separation'.[27] In light of the numbers, the accusation does not seem unfounded; the first Congress was graced by no more than two Muslim delegates.[28]

---

26 Charles H. Heimsath, *Indian Nationalism and Hindu Social Reform*, (OUP, 1964), p. 205.

27 P.N. Chopra, Ram Gopal, and M.L. Bhargava, *A Century of the Indian National Congress. 1885-1985* (Delhi: Agam Prakashan, 1986), p. 30.

28 One of the two was R.M. Sayani who later went on to become the Congress President.

Nevertheless, every annual Congress session witnessed loud denials, both by Muslim and non-Muslim delegates, of any alleged Muslim apathy towards the body. For example, Munshi Syed Abdul Aziz, a delegate from Nagpur, fulminated at the 1886 session of the Congress that 'it is ridiculous to pretend that the Mahomedans who have any sort of education are wanting in interest in this Congress…'[29] Malik Bhagwan Das from Dera Ismail Khan, Punjab, chimed in,

> '…And what is this that I see in one of the English papers that calls this a Hindu Congress? Why Hindu? Why not Mahomedan? Does it follow because a man is Hindu he does not represent Mahomedans as well as Hindus? *(Loud Cheers)*'[30]

When the Congress reconvened in Madras next year, Badruddin Tyabji dismissed at length the notion that Muslims have not taken to the organisation. He said as much during his Presidential address,

> 'Gentlemen, it has been urged in derogation of our character, as representative national gathering, that one great and important community—the Musalman community—has kept aloof from the proceedings of the last two Congresses. Now, Gentlemen, in the first

---

29 Indian National Congress Proceedings, Microfilm No. 1433, *Detailed Report of the Proceedings of the Second Indian National Congress Held at Calcutta on the 27th, 28th, 29th and 30th of December, 1886* (New Delhi: National Archives of India), p.109.

30 Ibid., p.106.

> place this is only partially true and applies only to one part of India, and is moreover due to certain special, local and temporary causes…
>
> …so far as general political questions affecting the whole of India—such as those which alone are discussed by this Congress—are concerned, I, for one, am utterly at a loss to understand why Musalmans should not work shoulder-to-shoulder with their fellow countrymen of other races and creeds…'31

Some novel publicity literature that the Congress issued in 1887 also tried to prove that the Muslims of India are in perfect concord with it. Composed as a Socratic dialogue of sorts, it was titled the *Tamil Catechism*. At one point in this text, the following question is posed to someone who is obviously meant to be a votary of the Congress,

> ***Q***: What Mahomedans? Why, somebody said that the Mahomedans had not joined the Congress. I did not know what the Congress was, and so I did not trouble myself about it, but certainly I heard this.
>
> ***A***: Well, eighty-three Mahomedans[32] came as delegates,

---

31 Indian National Congress Proceedings, Microfilm No. 1433, *Detailed Report of the Proceedings of the Third Indian National Congress Held at Madras on the 27th, 28th, 29th and 30th of December, 1887* (New Delhi: National Archives of India), p.72.

32 I counted sixty-five obviously Muslim sounding names in the delegate list of the year. That means that Muslim delegates made up 10.72 percent of the total number of delegates (606). Even if I assume that I made a mistake, the share of Muslim delegates will not exceed 13.69 percent of the total.

> and amongst them there were men like the Hon'ble Mr Jah Bahadur, the head of the great Mysore family, and Mr Badruddin Tyabji, till recently a member of the Bombay Council, who was a President of the third Congress, and many other distinguished and learned Mussalmans. The fact is that one eminent Mahomedan, Sir Syed Ahmed, did not choose to join, for reasons known to himself, and he and his immediate following having been foolish enough to abuse the Congress, having tried to set it about that the Mahomedans generally did not join, whereas the bulk of the intelligent Mahomedans all over the country did join and join heartily.[33]

However, despite all efforts, it appears that the Congress was unable to conclusively establish that Muslims are not indifferent to it. Almost a decade later, we find it still seeking acquittal from the charge of not representing India's Muslims. R. M. Sayani (1847-1902), elected the Congress President in 1896, argued that it was a myth that the Muslims were against the Congress. He claimed that 'by far the largest part [of Muslims] do not know what the Congress movement is,' and

---

33 Indian National Congress Proceedings, Microfilm No. 1433, *Detailed Report of the Proceedings of the Third Indian National Congress Held at Madras on the 27th, 28th, 29th and 30th of December, 1887,* 'Appendix II, English Translation of the Tamil Catechism of the Indian National Congress by M. Viraraghava Chariar, B.A'. (New Delhi: National Archives of India), p.203.

those opposed to the Congress formed only an 'infinitely small class of persons'.[34]

Curiously, when we compare what Tyabji and Sayani had to say on the Muslims' attitude towards the Congress, we find that they both concede that at least a section of them were rather unenthusiastic about it. The *Tamil Catechism* was honest enough to even name 'one eminent Mahomedan' who was hostile to the Congress. What could be the reason behind certain Muslims' lack of ardour for the Congress? As it appears to us, they failed to be keen about the Congress because of the kind of political reforms demanded by it.

At its very first session, the Congress had passed a resolution seeking legislative bodies on the elective principle for India.[35] This remained for many subsequent years its foremost

34 Indian National Congress Proceedings, Microfilm No. 1433. *Detailed Report of the Proceedings of the Twelfth Indian National Congress Held at Calcutta on the 28th, 29th, 30th and 31st of December, 1896* (New Delhi: National Archives of India), p.34.

35 That this Congress considers the reform and expansion of the Supreme and existing Local Legislative Councils, by the admission of a considerable number of elected members and the creation of similar Councils for the North Western Provinces and Oudh, and also for the Punjab essential; and holds that all Budgets should be referred to these Councils for consideration, their members being, moreover, empowered to interpellate the Executive in regard to all branches of the administration; and that a standing committee of the House of Commons should be constituted to receive and consider any formal protests that may be recorded by majorities of such Councils against the executive of the power, which would be vested in it, of overruling the decision of such majorities. [Indian National Congress Proceedings, Microfilm No. 1433, *Detailed Report of the Proceedings of the Fourth Indian National Congress Held at Allahabad on the 26th, 27th, 28th and 29th of December, 1888*, 'Appendix II, Summary of the Resolutions Passed at the First, Second and Third Congresses' (New Delhi: National Archives of India), p.203.]

demand. The existing Councils[36] were seen to be but shams, dominated by nominated members. Prominent leaders of the Congress, as it appears, considered political representation a most basic and natural right and, hence, waxed eloquent on it. Addressing the 1886 Congress, Dr Rajendralal Mitra termed political representation the 'cornerstone of all the topics of political discussion'.[37] Surendranath Bannerji (1848-1925), never too far from hyperbole, went on to term representative self-government the 'ordering of nature, the will of divine providence'.[38] Not to be left behind, in the same session, Madan Mohan Malaviya stressed the 'utility, the expediency, the necessity' of the introduction of representative bodies in India since he thought them to be the 'fundamental characteristic of a free government'.[39]

Nevertheless, there were a few who chose to differ. As the annual Congress session commenced in Calcutta in 1886, Nawab Abdul Latif's (1828-1893) Mahomedan Literary Society distanced itself from it. The Nawab expressed his displeasure with the Congress's programme in a letter he addressed to its Reception Committee. Among other things, referring rather

---

36 The Indian Councils Act of 1861 had established Imperial and Provincial Councils but all their Indian members at that time were nominated by the Viceroy and the British Crown.

37 Indian National Congress Proceedings, Microfilm No. 1433, *Detailed Report of the Proceedings of the Second Indian National Congress Held at Calcutta on the 27th, 28th, 29th and 30th of December, 1886* (New Delhi: National Archives of India), p.49.

38 Ibid., p.98.

39 Ibid., p.108.

obliquely to the Congress's demand for representative bodies, he said,

> The Mahomedan Literary Society, representing the orthodox Mahomedan community In India, which forms the bulk of the Mahomedan population, are not disposed to accept hastily (sic) proposals, however well meant, which have a tendency to revolutionise time-honoured institutions, and to bring about changes that are novel, and which they consider unsuited to the exigencies of India of today, and the various and conflicting interests in it.[40]

Syed Ameer Ali's (1849-1928) Central National Mohammedan Association (hereafter CNMA) too abandoned the Congress in 1886, immediately prior to its Calcutta Session. Ali had originally supported the Congress when it was launched in 1885. A couple of years later, in 1888, the CNMA's annual report clarified why it had severed ties with the Congress. It had done so, the report explained, because it was 'firmly convinced that the unqualified adoption of the programme of the Congress [would] lead to the political extinction of the Mohammedans'.[41] The CNMA, it said, was

40 Quoted in the *Bengalee*, 25 December 1886. Nehru Memorial Museum and Library, Microfilm No. 1042.

41 Ram Gopal, *Indian Muslims. A Political History. 1858-1947* (Bomaby, Calcutta, New Delhi, Madras, London, New York: Asia Publishing House, 1959), p. 76.

'willing to concede that the system of nomination by which the Councils of the Government are recruited is not always happy in its results'.[42] But it feared that in a country like India 'voting must take place by nationalities and creeds'.[43] Hence, the CNMA, the report declared, 'cannot believe that the introduction of representative institutions in this country in their entirety [would] be of advantage to the Mahommedans'.[44]

By far, the strongest disagreement with the Congress's agenda was issued from Aligarh. We see it being articulated very unambiguously in an unsigned article published in the *Aligarh Institute Gazette* on 23 November 1886. The first objection that the anonymous article raised was that 'India at present is very poor compared with European countries in the possession of highly educated classes'.[45] Thus, the *Aligarh Institute Gazette* insinuated that individuals qualified to fill the proposed representative bodies were simply not to be found in the country. But the bigger fear that it expressed was one of brute majoritarianism taking over India. Since the will of the more numerous was most likely to find expression in a parliament, the article imagined that 'probably the uneducated Hindu majority would forbid the killing of cow, reintroduce Sati and employ public money in building temples, higher

42 Ibid.

43 Ibid., pp.76-77.

44 Ibid., p.77.

45 See Shan Mohammad, ed., *The Aligarh Movement: Basic Documents. 1864-1898. Vol. III* (Meerut, New Delhi: Meenakshi Prakashan), p. 967.

education would cease, and the progress of the country would come to an end'.[46] Further, since it is also natural for a parliament to have conflicting parties, it was feared that Indians (unlike Englishmen) are most likely to form these along religious lines. 'In India,' the article argued, 'two sections of people are ready to hand, and two sections whose interests and prejudices constantly clash, and which differ in a far more radical way than any two parties in England…'[47] This made our anonymous author apprehensive about the feasibility of representative bodies in the Indian situation. This polemicist thought that they would only serve to exacerbate entrenched prejudices,

> …if at any future time there should be Parliaments with Hindus and Mohammedans sitting on two sides of the house, it is probable that the animosity which would ensure (sic) would far exceed anything that can be witnessed in England.[48]

The *Aligarh Institute Gazette* had sure taken its editorial cue from the patriarch of Aligarh, Syed Ahmed Khan. As we see, he had no doubts that representative bodies and the right to franchise would become instruments of majoritarianism

46 Ibid., p.968.

47 Ibid., p.969.

48 Ibid., pp.969-970.

in the Indian context. Addressing a gathering at Qaiserbagh, Lucknow, on 28 December 1887, he launched into the following fulminations,

> They [the Congress] want to copy the English House of Lords and the House of Commons. The elected members are to be like members of the House of Commons; the appointed members like the House of Lords. Now, let us suppose the Viceroy's council made in this manner. And let us suppose first of all that we have universal suffrage, as in America…And first. suppose that all Mahomedan electors vote for a Mahomedan member and all Hindu electors for a Hindu member, and now count how many votes the Mahomedan member has and how many the Hindu. It is certain the Hindu member will have four times as many because their population is four times as numerous. Therefore we can prove by mathematics there will be four votes for the Hindu to every one vote for the Mahomedan. And now how can the Mahomedan guard his interests? It would be like a game of dice, in which one man has four dice and the other only one.[49]

Later in the same speech, Khan termed the demands raised by the Congress 'these monstrous and unreasonable schemes…

49 Shan Mohammad, ed., *Writings and Speeches of Syed Ahmad Khan* (Bombay: Nachiketa Publications Limited, 1972), pp. 209-210.

which are disastrous for the country…'[50] Khan's stance was not unsurprising in light of what he had opined earlier. Already in 1883, he had declared that 'the system of representation by election means the representation of the views and interests of the majority of the population'.[51]

How valid were the fears of Indo-Muslim elites like Syed Amir Ali and Syed Ahmed Khan regarding representative institutions and electoral politics? In light of the local politics of the times, it seems like their apprehensions were not entirely unfounded. We have already seen in the previous chapter how Muslims mostly tended to receive the short end of the stick in municipal politics. Mainly due to their numerical advantage, Hindus dominated the local boards and used them to pursue their cultural objectives in the urban spaces—this seriously threatened the public hegemony of the Islamicate cultural paradigm. Not just this, it appears that municipal politics could also generate rather aggressive 'communitas' among Hindus causing them to conduct their public ceremonials with greater pomp and even deploy them against Muslim holidays. For instance, Francis Robinson writes that the Hindus of Agra 'began to refurbish and celebrate with vigour the festivals that clashed with Mohurram'[52] when the 1883 Municipalities' Act produced a local municipal board dominated by their coreligionists. Inevitably, 'the result of this vigorous assertion

50 Ibid., p. 213.

51 *Indian Muslims: A Political History*, p. 62.

52 *Separatism among Indian Muslims. The Politics of the United Provinces' Muslims. 1860-1923* (New Delhi: OUP, 1994 [Second Impression]), pp.79-80.

of religious interests' was for 'the parties of municipal politics to become increasingly religious parties'[53] in the United Provinces. The same trend has been observed in Punjab by Kenneth Jones. Echoing Robinson, she too suggests that 'an arena for communal competition' came into existence due to the introduction of local self-government in the province. As a consequence, the religious communities of Punjab—Sikhs, Hindus, and Muslims—now 'fought for the control of the new structures'[54] of local representation and governance. It does look like we are witnessing a situation when 'the indigenous religious communities' had been 'thrown into the turmoil of re-negotiating the power relations between themselves'[55] by the new franchise-determined local politics. This communal contest, we suggest, was now unavoidable as, in however limited a way, the cultural character of the public spaces could be influenced through the force of numbers. Further, the capture of public spaces might mean that a religious group is better positioned to influence the state, as it is in these 'intermediary realm[s] between the individual and the citizen' that 'the polity brings pressure to bear on the state' and 'most of the current

53 Ibid., p.80.

54 Kenneth Jones, *Arya Dharma: Hindu Consciousness in 19th-Century Punjab* (New Delhi: Manohar, 1989), p.63.

55 Shashi Joshi and Bhagwan Josh, *Struggle for Hegemony in India. 1920-47. Culture, Community and Power. Volume III. 1941*-47 (New Delhi: Sage Publications, 1994), p.193.

debates are located'.[56] Also, these 'intermediary realms' are the site of 'conundrums' such as 'how citizens help shape the values of the state' and 'the extent to which the state is seen to be obliged to protect the beliefs and values of the various citizens…'[57]

It seems safe to contend that the developments in the contemporary local arenas were shaping the political attitude of the Indo-Muslim elite and making them wary of the Indian National Congress and its reforms' agenda. After all, the Congress seemed to be bent on replicating at a national level the same very institutions—the franchise and representative bodies—that were distressing and marginalising the Muslims at local levels. The misgivings of the Indo-Muslim elite are thus understandable. It was never going to be easy for the Congress to deal with these misgivings because, as Mohammad Yusuf Abbasi writes, the introduction of 'the elective principle' in local self-government had caused,

> 'a profound change…in the outlook of the major communities. Questions arose as to how the elective principle should be applied in the particular circumstances of the Subcontinent. Should the interests of the Muslim minority be subordinated to the general

---

56 Sandria Freitag, 'Contesting in Public: Colonial Legacy and Contemporary Communalism' in David Ludden, ed., *Contesting the Nation: Religion, Community, and the Politics of Democracy in India* (Philadelphia: University of Pennsylvania Press, 1996), p. 212.

57 Ibid.

> will of the majority, without any reservation; or should the elective principle be re-adjusted to safeguard Muslim minority *vis-à-vis* the Hindu majority? In this, priorities of a fundamental nature were involved, what came first: Indian nationalism or Muslim nationalism?'[58]

To put it plainly, the 'elective principle' could be a very genuine impediment to the realisation of the idea of Indian nationhood that the Congress was purveying. We have seen that there was a fundamental irony to it—the Congress had postulated the Indian nation in purely 'civic' terms as well as a federation of religious and normative groups. The introduction in India of representative bodies based on the elective principle could mean that one constituent of this federation, namely, the Muslims, are permanently disadvantaged from the political and cultural points of view and relegated to second-class citizenship. This, in turn, might render the Indian nation that the Congress was trying to forge not a 'civic' entity—a union of equal citizens subject to a non-discriminatory government—but a political expression of Hindu society alone, the majority of the land. The Congress, thus, was faced with difficult choices—either it could cynically concede that Muslims would indeed play second fiddle to the religious majority in the political future it had envisioned for India, or it could extend special guarantees

58 Mohammad Yusuf Abbasi, *The Genesis of Muslim Fundamentalism in British India* (Publication Department: Indian Institute of Applied Political Research, 1987), p.73.

to the Muslims and acknowledge their distinct political interests as a minority.

What did the Congress do? Partly, it sought to disarm the Muslim opposition with platitudes. For example, Eardley Norton, an Anglo-Indian delegate from Madras, said as much at the 1887 annual Congress:

> We have been told, again, that in this matter [political representation] you are purely Hindu and Mahomedan. What can you conceive, gentlemen, more false (sic.) than that? Have our critics forgotten that we, as Europeans, even for the limited portion of our sojourn in India, are as deeply affected by questions of taxation and of legislation as any of yourselves, Mahomedan or Hindu?[59]

In other words, Norton was seemingly confident that Indian representative bodies would only give expression to the civic concerns relevant to the majority and minorities alike without fracturing along religious identities. On the other hand, Pandit Bishan Narain Dar, a delegate from Oudh, refused to believe that 'the introduction of representative Government in India [would] place the Mahomedans at the mercy of the Hindus, as the latter [would] form a great majority…'[60] Pandit Dar drew

59 Indian National Congress Proceedings, Microfilm No. 1433. *Detailed Report of the Proceedings of the Third Indian National Congress Held at Madras on the 27th, 28th, 29th and 30th of December, 1887,* p.90 (New Delhi: National Archives of India).

60 Ibid.

his optimism from the European example. 'In Europe, there may be Catholic interests and Protestant interests,' he pointed out, '...yet the existence of such interests has not prevented the success of representative institutions'.[61] Contending religious interests or loyalties, thus, as Pandit Dar saw, were not going to encroach upon the domain of political representation. In fact, according to him, political representation could actually serve as a potent means of reconciling any mutual aversion between religious groups. 'It is said,' he averred,

> 'that there is such hostility between Hinduism and Mahomedans as to render it [representative bodies] impossible...I say if this terrible antagonism did exist, even the representative institutions would do more than anything else to remove it.'[62]

The Muslim delegates too would be sometimes optimistic like Norton and Dar. For example, at the 1888 annual Congress Oomrao Mirza Hajrat, a resident of Delhi, confidently averred that 'Members elected [to the representative bodies] would carefully avoid anything that would create religious or caste prejudices...'[63]

The Congress, however, was not all platitudes. It was also

61 Ibid.

62 Ibid.

63 Indian National Congress Proceedings, Microfilm No. 1433. *Detailed Report of the Proceedings of the Fourth Indian National Congress Held at Allahabad on the 26th, 27th, 28th and 29th of December, 1888* (New Delhi: National Archives of India), p.91.

contemplating some substantive measure to permanently assuage the fears of the Muslim opposition. For instance, we come across Badruddin Tyabji writing a letter to the editor of the *Pioneer* newspaper after serving his stint as the President of the Congress. In this candid epistle, he owned up to what he felt was the chief reason behind the Muslims' distrust of the Congress. His coreligionists, he wrote, felt that,

> some anxiety lest at future Congresses resolutions that could not commend themselves to the Mussalmans as a body, might in virtue of the greater numerical strength of the Hindus be passed…

He was, however, not sitting idle but doing what he could to soothe this anxiety. In the same letter Tyabji confided that,

> in order to convince them, and others who share doubts…[he had] requested the General Secretary [A. O. Hume] to address all the standing Congress Committees whether they were willing that a rule should be passed, that in case of the Mahomedan delegates unanimously objecting to the introduction of our subjects or the passing of any resolutions, such subjects or resolutions should be thereupon dropped.[64]

In other words, Tyabji was urging the Congress to

64 Badruddin Tyabji Papers, Microfilm No. 1333 (New Delhi: National Archives of India). The letter did not bear a date, but it might have been written in early 1888, soon after the 1887 annual Congress session over which Tyabji presided.

acknowledge the Muslims as a distinct and special political interest group and grant them a veto of sorts.

Syed Ahmed Khan, however, was still unwilling to drop his hostility towards the Congress. He too dispatched a letter to the *Pioneer* and argued that the 'mere fact of any resolution being carried unanimously does not make the Congress a 'national' one'.[65] He pointedly refused to accept that the Congress is a 'national' political forum and warned that if Muslims joined the organisation 'they [would] suffer great misfortunes…'[66] Khan elaborated his stand further in a letter he addressed to Tyabji on 24 January 1888. 'We [the opponents of the Congress] do not mean,' he wrote, 'to retard the general progress of India or to prevent other people from enjoying rights for which they are qualified, even if we try to do so we cannot hope to succeed, but at the same time it is not obligatory on our part to run a race with persons with whom we have no chance of success'.[67] Along with the Congress's program, we again find the Syed questioning the 'national' credentials of the organisation. The Congress could not be 'national' and represent an Indian nation, he thought, due to the plain reason that no such thing existed.

> …I do not understand what the words 'National Congress' mean. Is it supposed that the different castes and creeds living in India belong to one nation, and

65 Hafeez Malik, ed., *Political Profile of Syed Ahmed Khan. A Documentary Record* (New Delhi: Adam Publishers and Distributers, 2006), p.377.

66 Ibid., p.379.

67 Badruddin Tyabji Papers, Microfilm No. 1335 (New Delhi: National Archives of India).

> their aims and aspirations are one and the same?...I object to every Congress in any shape or form whatever which regards India as one nation on account of its being based on wrong principles, viz., that it regards the whole of India as one nation.[68]

What made the Syed deny Indian nationhood? We suggest that it was because the Congress wanted this nation to be represented in legislative bodies in which, the Syed feared, the Muslims, being a minority, would be permanently disadvantaged. The Syed's opposition of Congress and his denial of Indian nationhood seem to stem from the same fear—the future (however unlikely) prospect of representative bodies being introduced in India.

Tyabji tried to reason with the Syed in a reply he wrote on 18 February 1888. He sought to allay the Aligarh patriarch's disapproval of the Congress by stressing that its existence is a mere practical requirement. 'In my view,' he wrote,

> the Congress is nothing more and should be nothing more than an assembly of educated people from all parts of India and representing all races and creeds met together for the discussion of only such questions as may be generally admitted to concern the whole of India at large.[69]

---

68 Ibid.

69 Badruddin Tyabji Papers, Microfilm No. 1333 (New Delhi: National Archives of India).

'It seems to me, therefore,' Tyabji concluded, 'that no one can object to a Congress of this kind unless he is of opinion that there are no questions at all which concern the natives of India at large'.[70] Having said this, the lawyer from Bombay assured Khan (it seems to us rather disingenuously) that even the Congress does not quite consider India a 'nation,'

> Your objection to the Congress is that 'it regards the whole of India as one nation.' Now I am not aware of anyone regarding the whole of India as one nation and if you read my inaugural address, you will find it distinctly stated that there are numerous communities or nations in India which had their peculiar problems of their own to solve, but that there were some questions which touched all those common unities and that it is for the discussion of these questions only that the Congress was assembled.[71]

Tyabji then proposed that if Khan at all wanted to cancel the brute logic of numbers, participation rather than keeping aloof was the solution. Muslims must bring to the Congress their own unique point of view and influence its choices. Interestingly, we see that Tyabji is suggesting that, if required, Muslims seek adjustments to how representatives are sent to the Legislative Councils. This was nearly two decades before the 'Simla Deputation'.

70 Ibid.
71 Ibid.

> But it is in our power with firm and resolute action to direct the course the Congress shall take, and my strong conviction is that the Mussulmans can by unified action confine the Congress to such topics only as they may deem desirable or safe for discussion. Take for instance the question of the Legislative Councils—if the Mussulmans as a body do not like that the members should be elected they could easily modify the propositions so as to suit their own interests. My policy, therefore, would be to act from *within* rather than from *without*.[72]

A few weeks ago, Tyabji had similarly pressed upon Syed Ameer Ali that Muslims ought not to isolate themselves politically. On 3 November 1887, Ali had written to Tyabji inviting him to a proposed conference of 'Mahomedan gentlemen of light and leading to discuss questions of importance really affecting the general interests of the Mahomedan community'.[73] Tyabji, however, was not enthused. In a reply he drafted on 3 December 1887, Tyabji said that he was all for the 'moral, social, and political advancement of the Mussulman community'.[74] But he believed that 'in regard to political questions at large the Mussulmans should make a common cause with their fellow

72 Ibid. The italicized words were underlined in the handwritten text.

73 Ibid.

74 Ibid.

countrymen of other creeds and persuasions'.[75] Tyabji ended the letter thus, '...it seems to me that our proper course is to join the Congress at Madras and to take a part in its deliberations from our peculiar standpoint'.[76]

While Tyabji was dealing with some prominent Indo-Muslims elites' clamant aversion for the Congress, there are indications that anxiety was building in the Congress camp. On 22 January 1888, A.O. Hume beseechingly wrote to Tyabji asking him to preside over the Congress once again. Hume conveyed to Tyabji that he has 'had letters on the Congress during the last few days' which said that if the Congress were to succeed it 'must again have a Mahomedan President' and that President must be Tyabji.[77] Hume imagined that this was the only way to disarm the Muslim opponents of the Congress. He reasoned with Tyabji that if he once again presides over the Congress as its President 'Syed Ahmed's tirades [would] have no effect on the north of India's Mahomedans...[78] History, however, tells us that Tyabji did not oblige Hume.

Hume wrote to Tyabji again on 20 October 1888, entreating him to attend the impending Congress. This was absolutely necessary, Hume told Tyabji, 'Because your defection would, no matter what the cause, cause us most serious discouragement'.[79]

75 Ibid.
76 Ibid.
77 Badruddin Tyabji Papers, Microfilm No. 1334 (New Delhi: National Archives of India).
78 Ibid.
79 Ibid.

Tyabji himself was not free from trepidation. Indeed, it seems that he was feeling quite a bit of it. This is evident from the reply he sent to Hume on 27 October 1888. 'You have no doubt,' Tyabji wrote, 'been watching the movement of the Mahommedans but still you are not so well acquainted with their feelings as I am'.[80] Tyabji had bad news for Hume. The Congress, Tyabji told Hume, was inspiring the 'hostile attitude of the Mahommedans, which is daily becoming more pronounced and apparent…' In Tyabji's view, things had come to such a pass that the cons of continuing with the Congress outweighed the pros. He, thus, wondered 'whether under the present circumstances, it is, (sic.) or not, wise for us to continue holding the Congress meeting *every year*'.[81]

Further, Tyabji warned Hume that the opponents of the Congress were growing in numbers since the 'Nizam… Salar Jung, Munir-ul-Mulk, Fateh Nawaz Jung and, above all, Syed Husain Bilgrami [had] joined the opposition led by Syed Amir Ali and Abdul Latif'.[82] Apparently, as we perceive, a broad coalition of the most prominent representatives of Indo-Muslim elite society was forming against the Congress. This made Tyabji conclude that 'an overwhelming majority of Mahomedans are against the movement'[83] that the Congress represents. The lawyer from Bombay thought that this took

80 Ibid.
81 Ibid.
82 Ibid.
83 Ibid.

away from the Congress its very *raison d'être*. 'If,' he reasoned with Hume, 'the Mussulman community as a whole is against the Congress—rightly or wrongly—does not matter—it follows that the movement ipso facto ceases to be *general* or *national* Congress'.[84] Further, Tyabji observed that the Congress was causing 'bitterness between the Hindus and Mussalmans...' In view of this state of things, Tyabji felt that it was preferable for 'the Congress to be prorogued, say for at least five years'.[85] He concluded the letter with the following suggestion,

> If at the end of the five years our prospects improve, we can renew our Congress. If not, we can drop it with dignity, conscious of having done our utmost for the progress of India and the fusion of different races into one.[86]

Hume replied to Tyabji on 5 November 1888 and tried to allay his fears. We find him conceding in his epistle that there were indeed parts of the country where the Congress was rather unpopular with the Muslims. 'All through Oudh and N.W.P.,' Hume wrote, 'we have ten Mahomedans to one that is against us...'[87] He also assured Tyabji that the situation elsewhere is a lot worthier of cheer. 'In Punjab,' for example, he found the Congress 'sweeping Syed Ahmed away'.[88] Hume was confident

84 Ibid.

85 Ibid.

86 Ibid. The italicized words were underlined in the handwritten text.

87 Badruddin Tyabji Papers, Microfilm No. 1333 (New Delhi: National Archives of India).

88 Ibid.

that 'within the next two or three years,' the Congress would have 'every single maulvi'[89] on its side. But before that could happen, the Congress was expected to take a significant initiative by these clerics. They demanded, informed Hume, that it pass 'some rule to the effect…that Government should always so arrange the nominations…as to equalise as nearly as possible the number of Mahomedan to Hindu members in the Councils'.[90] It looks like elements in the Muslim clergy already wanted Muslims to have political parity with the Hindus. As we shall see below, certain Muslims in the Congress too were to soon express this wish. Hume concluded by urging Tyabji to cease imagining that 'a large number of Mahomedans' are opposed to the Congress.[91]

In retrospect, it seems that Tyabji's fears were not put to rest. After 1888, the gentleman practically retired from the Congress. It is possible that, besides his failing health and the demands of the legal profession, his despondence might have been a reason why he chose to do so.

COMMUNAL VETOES, PROPORTIONAL REPRESENTATION, COMMUNAL PARITY, AND WEIGHTAGE

The Congress, apparently, was trying its best to accommodate the anxieties of the Indo-Muslim elite and circumscribe,

89 Ibid.
90 Ibid.
91 Ibid.

somehow, the inexorable logic of numbers. Months before engaging in correspondence with Tyabji, we find Hume attempting to devise, what seems to us, some effective means of mollifying and winning over the Congress's elite Muslim opposition. Seeking to institutionalise the rule Tyabji had suggested in his letter to the *Pioneer* newspaper, and, perhaps, also to garner the support of 'every single maulvi,' Hume dispatched the following missive to all the Standing Congress Committees on 5 January 1888,

> In the course of his conversations with numerous Mahomedan gentlemen, our late honoured President discovered that in the minds of those who have been holding aloof from the Congress movement, an apprehension lurked that the Hindus, being numerically strongest, might at some time press and carry in the Congress some resolution hostile to the Mahomedan interests.
>
> ...Now it is extremely desirable to render all such misconceptions impossible, by a definite rule on the subject...such a rule, if accepted, would completely obviate all remaining difficulties in the way of their [Muslims'] hearty cooperation in the [Congress] movement.[92]

92 Badruddin Tyabji Papers, Microfilm No. 1334 (New Delhi: National Archives of India).

'The rule' surfaced at the 1888 annual Congress in the form of the following resolution which was unanimously adopted,

> …that no subject shall be passed for discussion by the Subjects Committee or allowed to be discussed at any Congress by the President thereof, to the introduction of which Hindu or Mahomedan delegates, as a body, are unanimously, or nearly unanimously, opposed… thereon such resolution shall be dropped; provided that the rule shall refer only to subjects in regard to which the Congress has not already pronounced an opinion.[93]

As we see, the Congress, through the above resolution, conceded the idea of communal vetoes while also de facto admitting that religious loyalties and political points of view might legitimately coincide. This was, by all means, a watershed moment in the politics of nineteenth century India.

In 1889, the Congress took a further step to ensure that Muslims are not overwhelmed by the religious majority in the representative bodies of the future. Eardley Norton, an Anglo-Indian delegate from Madras, tabled a 'skeleton scheme' for council reform which demanded that no less than half the strength of the Imperial or Provincial Legislative Councils comprise elected members and that voters in each district elect

93 Indian National Congress Proceedings, Microfilm No. 1433. *Detailed Report of the Proceedings of the Fourth Indian National Congress Held at Allahabad on the 26th, 27th, 28th and 29th of December, 1888* (New Delhi: National Archives of India), p.171.

representatives to one or more electoral bodies 'according to the circumstance.' The resolution also contained the following clause,

> All representatives thus elected by all the districts included in the jurisdiction of each electoral body, to elect members to the Imperial Legislature at the rate of one per five million of the total population of the electoral jurisdiction and to their own Provincial Legislature at the rate of one per million of the said total population, in such wise that whenever the Parsis, Christians, Muhammedans or Hindus, as the case might be, elected to the Provincial Legislature, would not, so far as possible, bear a less proportion to the total number of members elected thereto, than the total number of Parsis, Christians, Hindus or Muhammedans, as the case might be, in such electoral jurisdiction, bore to its total population. Members of both Legislatures to possess certain qualifications and not to be subject to certain disqualifications.[94]

In simple language, the Congress was proposing that the principle of proportional representation of religious communities be adopted in India through electoral practice.

---

94 Indian National Congress Proceedings, Microfilm No. 1433. *Detailed Report of the Proceedings of the Fifth Indian National Congress Held at Bombay on the 26th, 27th and 28th of December, 1889* (New Delhi: National Archives of India), p.12.

As Norton explained, this was because India is a collection of 'vast varieties of creeds and men of different races' and a scheme must be submitted to the government to 'provide for the absolute protection of the minorities of this country'.[95] Affirming Norton's observation, Lala Lajpat Rai added that 'minorities, in whom…feeling of Indian brotherhood is not yet as fully developed' now ought not to have 'doubts and think themselves unrepresented'.[96] The Congress had breached yet another discursive frontier as it was desperately trying to bring around the Indo-Muslim elite. It had, so to speak, legitimised the notion that religious identities may be normally and rightfully expressed in electoral practice and, by extension, representative bodies. It had also, in the process, resolved the contradiction informing its vision of Indian nationhood, albeit in an unwelcome fashion. The Congress had tacitly admitted that the Indian nation as expressed in the proposed representative bodies would indeed be a federation of religious and normative groups and not an entity cohering around purely civic sentiments and concerns.

Unfortunately, the debate that ensued the tabling of the above resolution turned somewhat unseemly. Munshi Hidayat Rasul, a delegate from Oudh, rose and hinted that he is not completely in disagreement with the Muslim detractors of the Congress. He thought, as he put it, that they are not 'in the

95 Ibid., p.14.
96 Ibid., p.19

least'[97] the enemies of the Muslims who are with the Congress. Rasul, however, had a bigger surprise in store. He went on to claim that in the previous annual Congress, Pundit Ajudianath, a fellow delegate from his part of India, had assured him that Muslims would have parity in representation. He demanded that the Congress concede this principle of communal parity. Once it did so, Rasul promised the Congress sanguine prospects among Muslims,

> I assure that if you accept the principle of equality you will have on your side ninety per cent of Mussulmans from tomorrow and the remaining ten per cent from the day after tomorrow.[98]

A far more radical proposal came from Syed Wahid Ali Rizvi, a delegate from the North West Provinces. He demanded that

> ...if India is to be represented by her best and not by her inferior races, and in accordance with these views and out of regard to the past glories of...[an] ancient race, I call upon the Congress to rule, not that there shall be as many Mahomedans as Hindus in the councils but that there shall always be three times as many Musalman as Hindu members.[99]

97 Ibid., p.27.
98 Ibid., p.28.
99 Ibid., p.29.

After Rizvi finished his impassioned speech, Ali Mohamed Bhimjee from Bombay rose to address the Congress. On behalf of Rizvi, he tabled an amendment to Norton's resolution,

> The speaker who preceded me has proposed an amendment…'Provided that the number of Mahomedan members shall always be equal to that of the Hindus, in both the Imperial and Provincial Councils.'[100]

Bhimjee assured the Congress that the 'demand has not been proposed with any distrust towards the Hindu majority' and it only appeals to their 'spirit of tolerance'.[101]

There were, of course, Muslim delegates who provided saner counsel. Hamid Ali Khan from Oudh warned his coreligionists that they must not 'spread disunion and disagreement' as 'no good can come out of demanding, or even obtaining, an equal number of Mussulman members on the Legislative Councils'.[102] By broadcasting such ambitions, Khan thought, Muslims would only 'rouse suspicion' regarding their 'relations with and intentions towards' their 'Hindu brethren'.[103] Mir-uddin Ahmed Balkhi from Bihar reminded his fellow Muslim Congressmen that they have assembled 'for one common object, and that object is a secular and not religious one'.[104]

---

100 Ibid.
101 Ibid.
102 Ibid., p.30
103 Ibid.
104 Ibid.

Apparently, despite the pleadings of Hamid Ali Khan and Mir-uddin Ahmed Balkhi, there were still Muslim delegates who thought that demanding parity in representation is not a wholly untenable idea. Thus, Munshi Nasiruddin Ahmed, a delegate from Banaras, rose in the wake of the two gentlemen to make the same demand as Munshi Hidayat Rasul but in a significantly more moderate language,

> ...we Mussalmans shall rejoice if, as a mark of your confidence in and love for us, you were to concede to us an equal number of representatives in the Councils. But none of us, at least none who are sane and in the possession of our full senses, are going to pretend that we have any right to this.[105]

An amendment to Norton's resolution, a clause that would have given Muslims parity in representation with non-Muslims, was now put to vote, first only among the Muslim delegates. Interestingly, an overwhelmingly large number of them abstained from voting. This was because, as the anonymous compiler of the *Detailed Report of the Proceedings of the Fifth Indian National Congress* tells us, they 'could not vote for what they felt to be unreasonable, neither did they like to oppose what was so vehemently urged by several of their co-religionists, and what was, if could be conceded, so manifestly complementary to their community'.[106] Eventually, only thirty-

105 Ibid.

106 Ibid., p.32.

nine Muslim delegates out of the two hundred and thirty-odd present voted and the amendment was defeated, twenty-three votes to sixteen. Following this, it was unanimously defeated by the non-Muslim delegates.

One might be tempted to dismiss these Muslims who absurdly demanded that the Congress concede parity of representation between Hindus and Muslims as oddballs unworthy of serious consideration. This is, however, inadvisable. This is because, barring Bhimjee, they came from North India and, presumably, were representatives of Indo-Muslim elite society. The title 'Munshi' (scribe) borne by them, after all, appears to indicate that they were *ashrāf* who belonged to the Muslim service elite. Thus, there were already in the nineteenth century Indo-Muslim elites who were thinking in terms of political parity between Hindus and Muslims to nullify the Hindu advantage in numbers. This is extremely crucial, since this is so redolent of the 'two-nation theory'—at its heart was also the idea that Muslims ought to have political parity with Hindus. Based on what unfolded at the 1889 annual Congress, it looks like one may trace the discursive rudiments of the 'two-nation theory' in the nineteenth century, especially in the light of Syed Ahmed Khan's dismissal of Indian nationhood.

The notion that Muslims, due to their unique value, are entitled to weightage in political representation seems to go back to the nineteenth century as well—we saw it being expressed (rather crudely) by Syed Wahid Ali Rizvi. Two decades later, the Morley-Minto reforms conceded Rizvi's wish to an extent when they provided for a total Muslim representation of 40.7% on the Viceroy's Council—this was 'well in excess of the actual proportion of Muslims in the population' of India at that time[107] (a little over twenty-four per cent). Muslims were similarly over represented on the Imperial Legislative Council with nearly thirty per cent of the elected seats beings allotted to them. Again, the Lucknow Pact, signed between the Congress and the All-India Muslim League in 1916, granted weightage to Muslims in the provinces in which they were in a minority (though this was in lieu of reducing the number of Muslim seats in the Muslim majority provinces).[108] We do not know if Rizvi lived through the Morley-Minto reforms and the Lucknow Pact. In case he did, he probably might have been pleased to see the colonial establishment and the Congress seemingly acknowledging 'that Islam has something in it which is not to be found in other religions' and it 'entitles the followers of Muhammad to special consideration'.[109]

Finally, it is interesting to note individual Indo-Muslim elites, both without and within the Congress, confidently talking about Muslims as a generic, seemingly undifferentiated, social mass and presuming to speak on their behalf. Was this on account of the Islamic 'reform' efforts of the first half of the nineteenth century? Perhaps. We are tempted to hazard this guess. This is since, as is argued, puritanical Islamic reform

---

107 Farzana Shaikh, *Community and Consensus in Islam. Muslim Representation in Colonial India. 1860-1947* (Melbourne: CUP, 1989), p.152.

108 Ibid., p.171.

109 Ibid., p.154.

generated a more socially and culturally cohesive Indian Muslim society while also, as it seemed to us, letting the Indo-Muslim elite assume a leadership role in its midst.

'THE ONLY TRUE INTERPRETER BETWEEN THE RULER AND THE RULED'

In 1890, the essentials of the second Indian Councils Act had begun to assume shape. When the Congress met in Calcutta for its annual session at the end of the year, it yet again sought to diffuse the apprehensions of its opponents through florid rhetoric. Lal Mohan Ghose, a local delegate, remarked that 'the leaders of those communities as have been sounding the note of alarm' must not expect 'dangers from a scheme to be drawn up by the Government of India itself'.[110] Ghose asked these sceptics to trust the government 'to safeguard to the fullest extent the legitimate rights and interests of all the minorities of this country'.[111] He, we note, was seeking to assuage the fears

---

110 Indian National Congress Proceedings, Microfilm No. 1433. *Detailed reports of the Proceedings of the Sixth Indian National Congress Held at Calcutta on the 26th, 27th, 29th and 30th of December, 1890* (New Delhi: National Archives of India), p.15. Ghose had risen to propose the following resolution - That the Congress, having considered the draft bill recently introduced into Parliament by Mr. Charles Bradlough, entitled 'An Act to Amend the Indian Councils Act of 1861,' approves the same as calculated to secure a substantial installment of that reform in the administration of India, for which it has been agitating, and humbly prays the Houses of Parliament of the United Kingdom of Great Britain and Ireland to pass the same into law; and further that its President, Mr. Pherozeshah Mehta, is hereby empowered to draw up and sign on behalf of this assembly, a petition to the House of Commons to the foregoing effect, and to transmit the same to Mr. Charles Bradlough for presentation thereto, in due course. (Ibid., p.14)

111 Ibid.

of the Indo-Muslim elite by evoking the colonial regime and its sense of justice. Pherozeshah Mehta tried to assuage these fears too, but he rested his hopes on the good sense of those wielding the franchise. During his Presidential speech, he claimed that,

> experience has shown that in a preponderating Hindu electorate it does not happen that Hindus are elected; as so many other, besides racial forces and interests concur in influencing the selection.[112]

Nevertheless, it looks like the Congress was by now getting somewhat chary of discussing the fraught matter of communal representation. The resolution tabled by Ghose, for example, while urging the British parliament to expedite political reform, did not make even an indirect reference to it. This was much to the liking of Pandit Bishan Narayan Dar, who thought that the Congress ought to leave 'these matters of detail in the hands of Government'.[113] Such an attitude, he thought, would 'save the Congress from a good deal of odium and throw upon the government the entire responsibility of adjusting the conflicting interests, so-called, of the Hindu and Muhammadan communities'.[114]

112 Ibid., p.7.
113 Ibid., p.20.
114 Ibid.

At its 1891 annual session, the Congress passed another resolution demanding representative bodies for India.[115] Throughout these three days, it discussed neither communal representation nor the fact that there were points of view opposed to representative bodies for India. The Congress simply skirted these issues. The next annual Congress, on the other hand, was witness to an unfortunately arrogant dismissal of Syed Ahmed Khan. The culprit was Pandit Bishumbhar Nath. Speaking as the Chairman of the Congress's Reception Committee, he briefly and mockingly dwelt upon the opposition to representative bodies emanating from Aligarh. Sir Auckland Colvin (1838-1908), the Lieutenant-Governor of the North-Western Provinces and Oudh, had recently stopped by at the Mohammedan Anglo Oriental College and given a speech endorsing the view that representative bodies are unsuitable for India. Suspecting that Sir Colvin has borrowed 'a great deal of his politics from the political teachings of the venerable sage there' (presumably Sir Syed Ahmad Khan), Pandit Nath

115 That this Congress reaffirms the conclusion arrived at by all the previous Congresses, viz., that India can never be well or justly governed, nor her people be prosperous or contented, until they are allowed, through their elected representatives, a potential voice in the Legislature of their own country, and respectfully urges the people of Great Britain and Ireland, whose good-will towards India it gratefully recognizes, to permit no further delay in the concession of this just and necessary reform. (Indian National Congress Proceedings, Microfilm No. 1433, *Detailed report of the Proceedings of the Seventh Indian National Congress Held at Nagpur, on the 28th. 29th. and 30th December 1891* (New Delhi: National Archives of India), pp.16-17.)

peremptorily declared that the Congress 'need not now care much for such imbecile platitudes'.[116] Later, a unanimous resolution on the soon to be passed Indian Councils' Act was adopted at the same annual session. It regretted that the Act did not concede the electoral principle in the administration of India.[117]

The Indian Councils Act was passed by the British Parliament in 1892. When the Congress convened its annual session at Lahore later that year, R.N. Modholkar (1857-1921) summed it up for those in attendance. 'It did not give…exactly what the [the Congress] wanted,' he regretted, yet, he said,

> it gave us this much. In the Act there is permission, so to say, granted to the viceroy to select or elect persons for nomination to his Council. By the Act, there is no right of election as such granted, but in the nominations the Viceroy has to make, he is empowered to make

116 Indian National Congress Proceedings, Microfilm 1433, *Detailed report of the Proceedings of the Seventh Indian National Congress Held at Allahabad, on the 28th, 29th, and 30th December 1892* (New Delhi: National Archives of India), p.8.

117 That the Congress, while accepting in a loyal spirit the Indian Councils Act recently enacted by the Parliament of Great Britain, as explained by the present Prime Minister, with the assent of the then Under-secretary of State for India, that it is intended by it to give the people of India *a real living representation* in the Legislative Councils, regrets that the Act does not, in terms, concede to the people the right of electing their own representative to the Council, and hopes and expects that the rules now being prepared under the Act, will be framed on the lines of Mr. Gladstone's declaration in the House of Commons, and will do adequate justice to the people of this country; further, that it prays that these rules may be published in the official Gazettes, like other proposed legislative measures, before being finally adopted. (Ibid., p.27.)

rules with the sanction of the Secretary of State, and in making those rules a wide discretion is left to him.[118]

Modholkar did not at all dwell on the fact that certain people out there were staunchly opposed to the introduction of the 'right of election' in India, if that is what he meant by the Viceroy using his 'wide discretion'. The Congress was now giving up even alluding to the perspective of its critics, leave alone engaging with it.

The Congress had never been particularly successful in attracting Muslims. However, as the 1890s began, it seems like its popularity simply plummeted among them. In terms of percentages, barring one exceptional year, Muslim participation at the annual Congress sessions now nearly halved in comparison to the 1880s.[119] It might be because, as the *Detailed Reports of the Proceedings* reveal, the Congress

118 Indian National Congress Proceedings, Microfilm 1433, *Report of the Ninth Indian National Congress Held at Lahore on the 27th, 28th, 29th and 30th of December*, 1893 (New Delhi: National Archives of India), p.45. The Indian Councils Act of 1892 merely increased the size of the existing councils and allowed certain interests groups such as chambers of commerce or *zamindars*, along with district boards and municipalities, to recommend members to the provincial councils.

119 See Appendix. The exceptional year was 1899 when the annual Congress assembled at Lucknow and was attended by more than three-hundred Muslim delegates. As seen by Pundit Bishan Narayan Dar, this was because Hindu-Muslim relations were extremely cordial in Lucknow. Nevertheless, in his own admission, about fifty Muslims notables of the city had earlier petitioned the Lieutenant-Governor of the Province to keep the Congress from meeting there.
See A. M. Zaidi and S. Zaidi, eds., *The Encyclopaedia of the Indian National Congress. Volume Three: 1896-1900. Gathering Storms* (New Delhi: S. Chand & Company Ltd., 1977), pp.437-438.

discussed political representation a lot less than it had done in the 1880s. When it at all did so, it studiously avoided engaging its opponents. For instance, the Congress discussed the 1892 Act at both the 1893 and 94 annual sessions, but without ever mentioning the misgivings of the Indo-Muslim elite regarding the introduction of representative bodies and the electoral principle in India. The Congress simply refused to venture into this territory for the rest of the 1890s.[120] As we saw above, Sayani did allude to the 'Muslim question' in 1896 during his Presidential address, but it was only to admonish the Muslim opponents of the Congress, not to engage with them. They too, on their part, cold-shouldered the Congress.

The Congress was also implicitly a party to the Hindu cultural assertion surveyed in the previous chapter. For instance, prominent cow protection activists like Lala Murli Dhar and Swami Ala Ram were associated with it.[121] This is unlikely to have boded well from the Muslim point of view. Pandit Madan Mohan Malaviya too was known to be sympathetic to the activities of the cow protection *sabhās*.[122] Besides, as we have seen, he was a publicist championing the cause of Hindi-Nagari. Bal Gangadhar Tilak was a full and proper member of

120 John R. McLane seems to agree with us. 'Between 1889 and the Muslim delegation's request at Simla in 1906 for separate electorates,' he says, 'the Congress made no major attempts to attract or open discussion with the Aligarh Muslims, who continued to be the best organized Muslim opposition to the Congress.' See *Indian Nationalism and the Early Congress*, p. 112.

121 Ibid., p.305.

122 Ibid., p.307.

the Poona cow protection society, 'although he never seems to have been very active'.[123] Sometimes, cow protection activism and the Congress organisation seemed to overlap formally. To give an example, after the conclusion of the 1891 annual session of the Congress at Nagpur, the local *gauraksh ni sabh* conducted a large meeting at its pavilions. It was attended by the Congress delegates.[124] Naturally, when massive cow protection riots broke out in 1893, Muslim alienation from the Congress was further 'strengthened'. [125] In light of this situation, it seems but natural that the Indo-Muslim elite were keeping aloof from the Congress, perhaps even more so since attempts were afoot at Aligarh to forge a Muslim alternative to it. The United Patriotic Association had been established by Sir Syed in 1888. Its declared objective was to 'remove those bad feelings from the hearts of the Indian people which the supporters of the Congress are stirring up throughout the country…'[126] Sir Syed followed up with the Mohammadan Anglo-Oriental Defence Association of Upper India in 1893. It was an openly partisan body and meant 'To protect the political interests of Mahomedans by representing their views before the English people and the Indian government'.[127] A distinct Muslim point

123 Ibid., p.306.

124 Sekhar Bandyopadhyay, *From Plassey to Partition. A History of Modern India* (Orient BlackSwan, 2022 [Second Edition]), p.242.

125 Sumit Sarkar, *Modern India. 1885-1947* (New Delhi: Macmillan India Ltd., 1983), p.94.

126 *The Aligarh Movement: Basic Documents. 1864-1898*, p.907.

127 Ibid., p.1042

of view, both addressing and articulated by the Indo-Muslim elite, had begun to emerge in all-India politics.

The Congress, on the other hand, went on to unilaterally assume the role of the sole representative of the Indian nation. For example, speaking as the Chairman of the Reception Committee at the 1900 annual session, Kali Prasanna Ray smugly termed the Congress 'the only true interpreter between the ruler and the ruled'.[128] The Congress had found the line to which it was to tenaciously cling right up to the partition of the Indian Subcontinent in 1947. Perhaps, by now, it had given up on active efforts at 'building bonds'. The Congress had come to a point when it cynically sought to 'mend cleavages' by simply ignoring them or pretending that they did not exist.

ON THE WAY TO 1906

As a new century dawned, Muslims continued to be lukewarm towards the Congress. Similarly, just as earlier, the annual Congress sessions were witness to the airing of platitudes that sought to glibly gloss over the relative absence of Muslims. For example, someone named Chistie said as much in Calcutta, at the 1901 annual session of the Congress,

> Gentlemen, it is said that Mahomedans are not prominent in the Congress. Well, where the

128 Indian National Congress Proceedings, Microfilm No. 1434, *Detailed Report of the Proceedings of the Sixteenth Indian National Congress Held at Lahore on the 27th, 28th and 29th of December, 1900* (New Delhi: National Archives of India), p.6.

> Mahomedans are prominent? Are they prominent in the Imperial Legislative Council, are they prominent in the Judicial Service, are they prominent as good scholars? That is the cause, that we are backward in education and backward in all movements that lead to progress and education.[129]

In other words, Chistie thought that Muslims were not numerous in the Congress since they were not numerous in any walk of life. As he understood, Muslims' small numbers in the Congress reflected their general backwardness and, apparently, did not necessitate alarm. On the other hand, addressing the same session, Surendranath Banerjee took eloquent satisfaction at the sight of the handful of Muslims whom the Congress had indeed attracted. He was sure that this boded something truly momentous,

> We Hindus rejoice to find that our Mahomedan fellow subjects have shaken off their political torpor (*Cheers*). The apathy which paralysed their energies has given place to serious reflection on their present political situation. A visible wave of unrest is agitating the Mahomedan community of India. Out of a total number of one

129 Indian National Congress Proceedings, Microfilm No. 1435, *Detailed Report of the Proceedings of the Sixteenth Indian National Congress Held at Calcutta on the 26th. 27th and 28th of December, 1901* (New Delhi: National Archives of India), p.81.

> thousand delegates attending the Congress there are so many as 100 Mahomedan delegates.[130]

With the benefit of hindsight, we of course know that Banerjee's optimism was misplaced and rather desperate. Perhaps, as he stood addressing the Congress, 'unrest' was indeed 'agitating' the Indian Muslims, or, at least, a section thereof. But it definitely did not drive them in the direction of the Congress. Instead, within five years, a number of the Indo-Muslim elites were to choose a course that would formalise their status as a distinct political interest all the way till 1947.

Presumably, Muslims remained indifferent towards the Congress since it continued with its 'monstrous scheme'—that of seeking representative bodies for Indians. As a matter of fact, it was now raising this demand with greater confidence and urgency. For example, the Congress passed a lengthy resolution at its 1904 annual session asserting that 'the time has arrived when the people...should be allowed a larger voice in the

130 Ibid., p.147. Our list shows the number to be 74, forming 8.25% of the total. (See Appendix)

administration and control of the affairs of their country'.[131] A little had been achieved, but now it was time for more. V. Krishnaswami Iyer from Madras called the reforms of 1892 a 'great and important change'[132] but also wondered 'whether the time has not come when another step may not be taken...'[133] Seemingly, this was because some numbers of Indians were now intellectually groomed enough to be able to occupy political office. As Jehangir B. Petit (1879-1946) put it,

> The desire to have 'representation' is the natural and legitimate outcome of a liberal education, such as we have been receiving in India....[134] We have now learnt to know what is good forms and what is bad: and have become a tremendous force in Indian society and there is no wonder that we are already knocking loudly at the

---

131 Indian National Congress Proceedings, Microfilm No. 1435, *Report of the Twentieth Indian National Congress Held at Bombay on the 26th, 27th and 28th December* 1904 (New Delhi: National Archives of India), pp.179-180. The full text reads thus: That in the opinion of the Congress, time has arrived when the people of this country should be allowed a larger voice in the administration and control of the affairs of their country by (a) The bestowal on each Province or Presidency of India of the franchise to return at least two members to the English House of Commons. (b) An enlargement of both the Supreme and Provincial Legislative Councils – increasing the number of non-official members therein and giving them the rights to divide the Council in all financial matters coming before them – the Head of the Government concerned possessing the power of veto. (c) The appointment of Indian representatives (who shall be nominated by the elected members of the Legislative Councils) as Members of the India Council in London and of the Executive Councils of the Government of India and the Governments of Bombay and Madras.

132 Ibid., p.181.

133 Ibid., p.182.

134 Ibid., p.192.

> door for some share in the responsible government of our native land.[135]

The next year, G. K. Gokhale (1866-1915), the President-elect, spelt out exactly what measures in matters of political representation the Congress wanted the colonial administration to implement. He demanded a reform of the Legislative Councils 'raising the proportion of elected members to one-half requiring the budgets to be formally passed by the Councils and empowering the members to bring forward amendments...' Further, Gokhale sought veto powers for the Presidents of the Councils and an increase in the number of elected members of the twenty-five-member Viceroy's Council from five to twelve.[136] Very likely hearkening to the resolution it had passed back in 1889, the Congress was perhaps not unwilling to concede the communal criterion in political representation. For example, we see the old Congress hand A.M. Bose (1847-1906) declaring that if it is 'deemed necessary' he would 'admit the element of sectional representation allotting to different communities or interests a certain minimum representation in the Local Councils'.[137]

135 Ibid., p.194.

136 Indian National Congress Proceedings, Microfilm No. 1435. *Report of the Proceedings of the Twenty-first Indian National Congress Held at Benaras on the 27th, 28th, 29th and 30th December, 1905* (New Delhi: National Archives of India), p.12.

137 Ibid. Appendix C, p. viii.

Meanwhile, a favourable political wind had begun to blow. Lord Minto (1845-1914) replaced Lord Curzon (1859-1925) as the Viceroy of India in 1905. He and the Secretary of State, Lord Morley (1838-1923), we learn, were 'determined' to win over the moderate Indians to a 'policy of association in the Government of India'.[138] Thus, over May and June 1906, the latter discussed with Gokhale reforms in the Secretary of State's Council, the executive councils of the Viceroy and Governors, and the legislative councils as demanded by the Congress.[139] Subsequently, on 20 July 1906, Lord Morley declared in the House of Commons his willingness to consider Indian political reforms if the initiative is taken by the Government of India.[140] This had to trigger a reaction at Aligarh.

On 4 August, Nawab Muhsin-ul-Mulk (1837-1907), the secretary of the Aligarh College, wrote to William Archbold (1865-1929), its then Principal. He was fearful that 'If the new rules now to be drawn up introduce 'election' on a more extended scale, the Mohammedans will hardly get a seat and no Mohammedans will get into the Councils by elections.' Interestingly, the Nawab also confided in Beck that certain 'young educated Mahomedans seem to have a sympathy for the "Congress"' and disappointment with the government may produce 'a greater tendency in them to join the Congress'.[141]

138 See Peter Hardy, *The Muslims of British India* (CUP, 1998), p. 153.

139 Ibid.

140 Ibid., pp.153-154.

141 As quoted by Hardy, p. 154.

It is possible that he was referring to the 'young [Muslim] gentlemen of progressive tendencies'[142] in the United Provinces. Apparently, they were getting increasingly disillusioned with the colonial administration and its putative sympathy for Muslims. Unhappy with the Nagari Resolution of 1900 and Muslims' continued inability to successfully cope with the principle of election, these youths were (rather desperately, it seems) threatening to go over to the Congress.[143] Perhaps, they wanted to bring to the Congress the 'peculiar' Muslim point of view—as Badruddin Tyabji had once urged Syed Ahmed Khan and Syed Ameer Ali to do. As Muhsin-ul-Mulk read the situation, some significant demonstration was required to assure them that the colonial state was not indifferent to the concerns of Muslims. The nervous Nawab thus asked Archbold whether the Viceroy might be amenable to receiving a Muslim deputation. Lord Minto, Peter Hardy tells us, read Muhsin's letter on 8 August (looks like Archbold forwarded it to him) and sent it to Morley with the following comment, 'I have not had the time to think over the advisability of receiving the proposed delegation but am inclined to do so'. On 10 August Archbold informed Muhsin that a Muslim delegation could indeed be received by Lord Minto.[144] This is how the 'Simla Deputation' was actualised.

The thirty-five-member delegation, led by Sir Sultan

142 *Separatism among Indian Muslims*, p.137.

143 Ibid., p.142.

144 *The Muslims of British India*, p. 154.

Mohammad Shah Aga Khan (1877-1957), claiming to be 'representing a large body of Mohammedan subjects of His Majesty the King Emperor in different parts of India'[145] waited upon the Viceroy on 1 October 1906. As these gentlemen put it, desire for a 'fair share' in extended representation provided in Municipalities, District Boards and Legislative Chambers along with 'some other matters of importance'[146] affecting the Muslim community had made them approach Lord Minto. Delicately evoking the memory of Mughal rule, the deputation politely urged the Viceroy to be mindful of the position Muslims had 'occupied in India a little more than hundred years ago…'[147] Perhaps, the delegation was seeking to obliquely tell the Viceroy that the political worth of Indian Muslims must not be weighed in terms of their numbers alone. Further, these, nearly three dozen, 'nobles, jagirdars, taluqdars, lawyers, zemindars, merchants and others' argued that Muslims are, after all, not as much a minority in India as they are believed to be. They, thus, declaimed that,

> The Mohammedans of India number, according to the census taken in the year 1901, over sixty-two millions or between one-fifth or one-fourth of the total population of His Majesty's Indian Dominions, and if reduction be made for the un-civilised portion of the community enumerated under the heads of animist and

145 *Indian Muslims. A political History. 1858-1947*, Appendix B, p. 329.
146 Ibid, p.330.
147 Ibid.

> other minor religions, as well for those classes which are ordinarily classified as Hindus but properly speaking are not Hindus at all, the proportion of Mahommedans to the Hindu majority becomes much larger.[148]

Having made the case for the political importance of Indian Muslims, the 'Simla Deputation' moved on to the matter of political representation. It pointed out to Lord Minto that 'representative institutions of the European type are new to the Indian people' and their adaption 'to the social, religious, and political conditions obtaining in India' warrants 'the greatest care, forethought and caution…' Unless due care and cautiousness was shown by the government in introducing representative institutions in India, these gentlemen feared, their 'national interests' would be placed 'at the mercy of an unsympathetic majority'. [149] It is interesting to note that they were already terming the Indian Muslims a 'nation' in relation to the Hindus. Moving on, the delegation made the gloomiest prognostication with regard to the prospects of Muslims if the elective principle is introduced in India. 'As for the result of elections,' the 'Simla Deputation' declared, 'it is unlikely that the name of any Mahommedan candidate [would] ever be submitted for the approval of Government by the electoral bodies as now constituted unless he is in sympathy with the majority in all matters of importance'.[150] These protagonists

148 Ibid.
149 Ibid., p.331.
150 Ibid.

of Muslim political interests also observed that 'in a good many places the Mahommedan tax payers are not adequately represented' on the Municipal and District Boards, as also that the representation of Muslims in these local bodies is not 'regulated by any guiding principle capable of general application, and practice varies in different localities'.[151]

The 'Simla Deputation' suggested the following to ensure adequate representation for Muslims at the local level,

> ...the local authority should in every case be required to declare the number of Hindus and Mahommedans entitled to seats on Municipal and district Boards, such proportion to be determined in accordance with the numerical strength, social status, local influence and special requirements of each community. Once their relative proportion is relatively determined, we would suggest that either community should be allowed severally to return their own representatives as is the practice in many towns in the Punjab.[152]

For the Legislative Councils this was the recommendation,

> Beginning with the Provincial Councils, we would most respectfully suggest that as in the case of Municipalities and District Boards the proportion of Mahommedan representatives entitled to seats should be determined and declared with regard to the important considerations

151 Ibid., p.333.

152 Ibid.

(those enlisted above)...the important Mahommedan landowners, lawyers, merchants and representatives of other important interests, the Mahommedan members of District Boards and Municipalities and the Mahommedan graduates of Universities of a certain standing, say five years, should be formed into Electoral Colleges and be authorised, in accordance with such rules of procedure as Your Excellency's Government may be pleased to prescribe in that behalf, to return the number of members that may be declared to be eligible.

With regard to the Imperial Legislative Councils whereon the due representation of Mahommedan interests is of vital importance, we crave leave to suggest (1) that in the cadre of the Council the proportion of the Mahommedan representatives should not be determined on the basis of the numerical strength of the community, and that in any case, the Mahommedan members should not be an ineffective minority; (2) that so far as possible, appointment by election should be given preference over nomination; (3) that for the purpose of electing Mahommedans, Mahommedan landowners, lawyers, merchants and representatives of other important interests of a status to be subsequently determined by Your Excellency's Government, Mahommedans of

> the Provincial Councils and Mahommedan fellows of Universities should be invested with electoral powers to be exercised in accordance with such procedure as may be prescribed by Your Excellency's Government in that behalf.
>
> An impression has lately been gaining ground that one or more Indian Members may be appointed to the Executive Council of the Viceroy. In the event of such an appointment being made, we beg that the claims of Mahommedans in that connection may not be overlooked.[153]

In his rejoinder, Lord Minto assured the delegation that he is 'entirely in accord' with their observation that, in their current form, 'electoral bodies cannot be expected to return a Mahommedan candidate' unless he sacrifices his 'view' to that of 'a majority opposed to his own community…'[154] He was also, he said, 'firmly convinced' that 'any electoral representation in India would be doomed to mischievous failure which aimed at granting a personal enfranchisement regardless of the beliefs and traditions of the communities composing the population of this country'.[155] In the end, he urged the 'Mahommedan community' to 'rest assured that their political rights and

153 Ibid, p.334.
154 Ibid., p.338.
155 Ibid.

interests as a community [would] be safeguarded in any administrative reorganisation' that concerns him.[156]

Lord Minto kept his promise. Three years later, the Indian Councils Act of 1909, or the Morley-Minto reforms, had a 'special provision' for the representation of Muslims along with 'professional classes' such as landholders and European and Indian commercial people.[157] Muslims were granted a separate electorate and eight out of twenty-seven elected seats on the Imperial Legislative Council were reserved for them (amounting to, as we saw above, 'weightage' in representation). Further, Muslims were required to fulfil a 'considerably lower' income qualification to be eligible to vote in comparison to the Hindus.[158]

How credible ought we to regard the 'Simla Deputation'? Was it, in the way of what it said, reading out from a script prepared by the rulers? In other words, as has been claimed, was the 'Simla Deputation' a 'command performance' manipulated by the colonial state? Peter Hardy does not think so. In his view, it is 'almost certainly false'[159] to think that the 'Simla Deputation' was a performance string pulled by the British. On the contrary, Hardy regards the 'Simla Deputation' as the 'outcome of a marriage of convenience between British political necessity and upper-class Muslim interests—and those of the

156 Ibid.

157 *Modern India*, p.140.

158 Ibid.

159 *The Muslims of British India.*, p. 156

Muslims of the United Provinces above all others.'[160] Minto's response to the deputation was, Hardy argues, the 'logical outcome of British policy in India after 1857, namely that the British act as arbiters between substantial interests believed—or hoped—to be irreconcilable, and that safety for British supremacy lay in an alliance with the substantial landholding classes'.[161]

There were, as we saw, 'lawyers' and 'merchants' on the 'Simla Deputation'. But it was definitely, by and large, an initiative not of the urban professional and mercantile groups but the traditional Indo-Muslim elite, or the *ashrāf*. This is evidenced by the multiple types of land controllers—namely, 'jagirdars,' 'taluqdars,' and 'zemindars'—as well as the aristocracy ('nobles') it included. It seems, based on what Hardy says, that these Indo-Muslim elites and the colonial administration had found expedient allies in each other. By hearing out the 'Simla Deputation,' the colonial state was perhaps seeing itself balancing out the Hindu and Muslim positions in Indian politics, while also visibly succouring a potential prop to its authority, namely, the *ashrāf* preponderating as land controllers. The *ashrāf*, on the other hand, found the colonial state willing to heed their two decades old anxieties regarding the franchise and representative institutions and provide redress.

Shorn of all the verbiage and minutiae, what the 'Simla Deputation' said amounted to the demand that Muslims be

160 Ibid., p.158.
161 Ibid., p.159.

granted proportional representation on the communal principle (over-conceded with weightage by the 1909 reforms). More broadly, one might observe that the 'Simla Deputation' sought the 'constitutional recognition of the communal group as the principal unit of representation'.[162] This wish was apparently rooted in a denial of the notion that 'individuals could be free agents in politics'—they were seen as 'primarily members of religious groups…'[163] The Simla Deputation, thus, was a hugely consequential intervention in the politics of colonial India in the sense that it normalised and 'mainstreamed' the following points of view—that Indian Muslims are a distinct political interest on account of their religion alone, and that their exercise of political choices may be legitimately determined by their religious identity. Further, as we saw, the 'Simla Deputation' stressed a putatively unique historical worth of Indian Muslims by recalling Mughal rule—it is as though these Indo-Muslim elites were insinuating that they, and the broader society they claimed to represent, were specially entitled to political consideration and power because of the dominance they had hitherto collectively exercised. This is particularly significant in light of the fact that the Simla Deputation also termed the Indian Muslims a 'nation'. In effect, this could mean that their political demands are regardless of their actual numbers or share in the population of India. Now, if the

162 Farzana Shaikh, *Community and Consensus in Islam*, p.136.
163 Ibid.

Indian Muslims desired, they might seek parity or weightage in political representation, or even a territorial state. In other words, it seems like the Simla Deputation sought to ensure that Indian Muslims were not hindered by the minority appellation as they negotiated their political future with the Hindus and the colonial administration. As we know with hindsight, the All-India Muslim League, formed on the penultimate day of 1906, gradually brought to colonial politics each one of the Simla Deputation's perspectives and positions. The climactic outcome of this was the birth of Pakistan in 1947.

CONCLUSION

The only difference is this, that brother Gandhi has three votes and I have only one vote.[1]

—Muhammad Ali Jinnah

Partition was the bloody denouement to the problem of satisfactorily accommodating a large and, in parts, a hitherto dominant minority in an Indian iteration of representative democracy. We do not know if Jinnah had Syed Ahmed Khan's Qaiserbagh speech in mind as he stood addressing the epoch-making AIML session which concluded with the adoption of the, as we call it today, 'Lahore Resolution'. He, nevertheless, sounded like Khan's spirit was prompting him from the wings. What Jinnah essentially meant while grumbling about his 'brother' Gandhi's three votes and his one vote was that Hindu votes three times outnumbered the Muslim ones. In

1 Syed Sharifuddin Pirzada, ed., *Foundations of Pakistan. All-India Muslim League Documents. 1906-1947. Vol. II. 1924-1947* (Karachi, Dacca: National Publishing House, 1970), p.332. He made this remark in 1940, while addressing the Lahore session of the All-India Muslim League.

our eyes, this is so reminiscent of Khan complaining, back in 1887, about the unfairness of Hindu votes outnumbering the Muslim ones four to one if parliamentary democracy after the British fashion is introduced in India. Though not from their society, Jinnah had brought to the politics of late colonial India the Indo-Muslim elite's point of view with consummate efficiency. Consciously or otherwise, this remarkably smart Gujarati lawyer was venting an anxiety about franchise-based representative institutions that his (so to speak) clients had been suffering from for more than two generations. He, thus, over the course of his speech, ruled out the suitability of 'the Westminster model of parliamentary democracy in Indian conditions' as it would mean 'perpetual minority for Muslims and rule by the Congress, the pre-eminent party of Hindu majority'.[2]

Jinnah, as a matter of fact, categorically declared at Lahore that 'Musalmans are not a minority' but 'a nation by any definition'.[3] Apparently, he thought so because of the 'fundamental and deep-rooted differences, spiritual, economic, cultural, social and political' between the Hindus and Muslims.[4] Jinnah's verdict, thus, was that the two nationalities, 'divergent' despite 'a thousand years of close contact,' 'cannot at any time be expected to transform themselves into one nation merely by means of subjecting them to a democratic constitution and holding

2 Ayesha Jalal, *Self and Sovereignty. Individual and Community in South Asian Islam since 1850* (New Delhi: OUP, 2001), p.399.

3 *Foundations of Pakistan*, p.335.

4 Ibid, p.337.

them forcibly together by unnatural and artificial methods of British parliamentary Statutes'.[5] He termed the problem in India an 'international' rather than an 'inter-communal' one[6] and ruled out the Muslims ever accepting 'a Hindu majority government'.[7] It was as though Jinnah, consciously or otherwise, was paraphrasing and developing the 'Simla Deputation's' position—one might recall that they had termed the Indian Muslims a 'nation' while meeting with Lord Minto.

The aftermath of the Gujarati lawyer's speech was rather significant, to say the least. The next day the AIML passed a resolution, moved by the Bengali-Muslim leader Fazlul Haq, demanding 'that the areas in which the Muslims are numerically in a majority, as in the North-Western and Eastern zones of India, should be grouped to constitute Independent States in which the constituent units should be autonomous and sovereign'.[8] The foundations of future Pakistan were laid.

Subsequent to the Lahore session of the AIML, having elevated Indian Muslims to the status of a nation, we find Jinnah trying to circumvent the cold arithmetic of political representation with the selfsame manoeuvre we saw certain Indo-Muslim elites adopting at the 1889 annual session of Congress. Like the two Munshis—Hidayat Rasul and Nasiruddin Ahmed—Jinnah sought to ensure that Muslims enjoy equality

5 Ibid.
6 Ibid.
7 Ibid., p.338.
8 Ibid., p.341.

with Hindus in the way of political representation. Firstly, in July 1940, he made the AIML's participation 'in the proposed Executive Council' contingent on 'parity' with Congress. What Jinnah implied by this, we are told, was 'that such parity must also consist of a communal balance between Hindus and Muslims' on the basis of the 'League's exclusive claim to nominate Indian Muslims.'[9] Then, throughout the 1940s, he 'repeatedly and categorically' rejected the 'principles of arithmetic to the problem of representation'.[10] He claimed that the actual issue at hand is one of constitutionally recognising the claims of political nations and not managing the 'demands of shifting political patterns'.[11] Again, Jinnah caused the Simla conference to 'crash'[12] in 1945 by insisting on parity between Hindus and Muslims, or the AIML and the Congress. Thus, as we understand, Jinnah picked up the Pakistan idea, around since it was mooted by Chaudhary Rahmat Ali in 1933, to emancipate Indian Muslims from a 'minority discourse' and make them the equals of Hindus at the political negotiating table. According to Ayesha Jalal, 'Once the independence of Muslim states in the northwest and northeast [of India] had been conceded, Jinnah was prepared to consider making

9 Farzana Shaikh, 'Muslims and Political Representation in Colonial India: The Making of Pakistan,' *Modern Asian Studies*, 1986, Vol. 20, No. 3 (1986), p.550.

10 Ibid., p.548.

11 Ibid.

12 Sekhar Bandyopadhyay, *From Plassey to Partition and After. A History of Modern India* (Hyderabad: Orient BlackSwan, 2022 [Second Edition]), p.445.

arrangements with Hindustan'.[13] In this sense, Pakistan was a very logical emergence from the ambitions and anxieties we found certain Indo-Muslim elites expressing in the nineteenth century. Whether organised as one or multiple territorial states, Pakistan could give Indian Muslims political parity with Hindus, just what Munshi Hidayat Rasul and Munshi Nasiruddin Ahmed had wished to achieve. On the other hand, it could keep them from being, as Syed Ahmed Khan and Syed Ameer Ali had feared, a perpetually hamstrung minority in matters of political representation.

The idea of Pakistan was also organically rooted in the cultural anxieties of the Indo-Muslim elite. This is quite apparent in the way this would-be homeland for Indian Muslims was visualised by some of these elites. Take, for instance, this pamphlet titled *Pakistan* that came out in February 1940. It was authored by one Anis al Din Ahmad Rizvi[14] — very likely a *sharif,* since the name end 'Rizvi' indicates descent from Imam Ali. As it appears to us, Rizvi imagined Pakistan as a realm wherein Indian Muslims would find fulfilment as Muslims, being able to live as per the moral discourse of Islam. As Venkat Dhulipala puts it, in Rizvi's view, Indian Muslims 'could become totally free and reclaim their former greatness' only with the 'power and choice to set up the Islamic state and

13 *Self and Sovereignty*, pp.399-400.

14 See Venkat Dhulipala, *Creating a New Medina. State Power, Islam, and the Quest for Pakistan in Late Colonial North India* (New Delhi: CUP, 2017), p.194.

[living] according to the teachings of the Quran'.[15] For Rizvi, true religious freedom meant that Muslims should be able to organise their 'collective life according to Islamic principles'.[16] Presumably, this freedom, in his imagination, could be enjoyed by Indian Muslims only if they established Pakistan. The Raja of Mahmudabad, charged with popularising Pakistan among the Muslims of British India by Jinnah,[17] broadly expressed the same imagination of Pakistan as Rizvi. Apparently, the uppermost and lower rungs of *ashrāf* society were on the same page while filling out the details of the Pakistan idea. As the Raja understood, Pakistan was only the second attempt 'in all of Islamic history' to establish an Islamic state, the first was at the time of the Prophet in Medina.[18] An Islamic state, he held, would apply 'the unchangeable laws of Islam' prohibiting liquor and usury and levying *zakat*.[19] The Raja, as it seems, nurtured no doubts that the future state of Pakistan ought to uphold Islamic orthopraxis.

The Raja of Mahmudabad had not been set on an unattainable objective by the Quaid-i-Azam. The *ashrāf* imagination of Pakistan clearly resonated with large numbers of Indian Muslims. Dhulipala, for instance, writes that Pakistan became the 'locus' of 'vigorous debate and discussion in U.P. soon after the Lahore Resolution'.[20] It could have been only due

15 Ibid., p.198.
16 Ibid., p.200.
17 Ibid., p.209.
18 Ibid., p.210.
19 Ibid.
20 Ibid., p.244.

to the growing popularity of Pakistan in Indian Muslim society that the AIML secured a massive 87 per cent of the Muslim Seats (429 out of 492) in the 1946 provincial elections (which were a veritable referendum on Pakistan). As we see, the quick 'traction' that Pakistan came to enjoy in Indian Muslim society definitely had something to do with the greater social and cultural coherence it had attained due to the *ashrāf* initiated reform efforts in the first half of the nineteenth century. This phenomenon also, very likely, was owing to the fact that the *ashrāf*, while 'reforming' Indian Muslim society, had assumed a tangible leadership role in relation to it. The broad masses of Indian Muslims, on the other hand, might also have looked up to the *ashrāf* and been rather spontaneously willing to follow them. We ought to be mindful that when cultural conflicts, surveyed by us in the third chapter, caused violent clashes or rioting, it was the average Indian Muslims who bore the brunt of it. They, thus, it seems plausible to suppose, nurtured the same cultural anxieties as the Indo-Muslim elite. That is probably why, the Indian Muslim masses eventually consolidated behind Jinnah's 'autocratic leadership'[21] as they were as uncomfortable with the 'Hindu' aspects of Congress nationalism'[22] as the *ashrāf*—be it the veneration of Gandhi,

21 Judith M. Brown, *Modern India. The Origins of an Asian Democracy* (OUP, 1994), p.331.

22 Ibid., p.312.

the singing of Vande Mataram,[23] or the Wardha Scheme of Education that allegedly devalued Islamic heroes and the Urdu language.[24] It is also tell-tale, as we see, that the 'growing nexus' between the AIML and an 'influential section of the Deoband *ulama*' proved crucial for the former's 'growth as a mass organisation'.[25] So, the AIML began to gain in popularity in Indian Muslim society only after it allied with the purveyors of an extremely puritanical variant of Islam. This could only be because it had some sort of appeal for the demographic that the AIML addressed. We shall, thus, dismiss Paul R. Brass's claim that the elite segment of Indian Muslim society was cynically manipulating Islamic cultural symbols to preserve its political privileges.[26] On the contrary, the Indo-Muslim elite deployed Islamic cultural symbols in their politics because they provided a most obvious and logical connection between them and their flock. If the Muslim masses did not have an instinctive 'feel' for Islamic cultural symbols, Pakistan would not have gone from being a mad scheme to a reality on the world map in less than fifteen years. It did so because it rode on a tremendous wave

23 Ibid.

24 *Creating a New Medina*, pp.76-77.

25 Ibid., pp.95-96.

26 According to Paul R. Brass, 'The ideology of Muslim separateness did not flow necessarily and inexorably out of the objective differences between Hindus and Muslims, but of the uses which were made of those differences through the manipulation of symbols of Muslim unity and Hindu-Muslim separateness by an elite concerned to preserve its political privileges.' (See Paul R. Brass, *Language, Religion and Politics in North* India (Delhi: Vikas Publishing House, 1975), p.120).

of Muslim popular sentiment. As Joya Chatterji puts it, 'Even if Jinnah himself did not really want Pakistan, his followers certainly did…'[27]

What about the Congress? As we see, it began on the wrong foot by expressing an idea of Indian nationhood which clashed with its political programme. Largely made up of westernised urban professionals as it was, the Congress could not think of the Indian nation as a civilizational expression, regardless of all diversities. Instead, it thought of it as a congeries of seemingly discrete religious and normative units. In other words, the Congress arrived on the scene with a rather colonially derived notion of what the Indian nation was or could be. We have seen that the constituent units of the Indian nation, as understood by the Congress, were implicitly meant to be autonomous in terms of their values and mores. A peculiarly Muslim point of view against the Congress, and its imagination of nationhood, thus became feasible. Prominent Indo-Muslim elites feared that the introduction of franchise-based representative institutions in India, Congress's foremost demand in its early years, would be a calamity for them and broader Indian Muslim society. As we saw, the *Aligarh Institute Gazette* was very candid in wondering if Hindus might impose their cultural ways on the country through their domination of democratic institutions. The Congress was initially lax, even callous, in addressing the

27 *Bengal Divided. Hindu Communalism and Partition, 1932-1947* (CUP:1994), p.226.

cultural anxieties of the Indo-Muslim elites who opposed it. It erred, to start with, on the side of too little. Meanwhile, one must note that the Congress was itself dallying with Hindu cultural assertion. We observed the participation of Madan Mohan Malviya in the Hindi-Nagari agitation and certain other Congressmen in cow protection. Later, however, the Congress went to the extent of institutionalising communal vetoes (1888) and conceding communal representation on a proportional basis (1889) to placate its opponents among the Indo-Muslim elites. The Congress we might say, fully legitimised the peculiarly Muslim point of view that was opposing it. But while it did so, the Congress failed to address the core worries of its Muslim opponents. It never owned up to the cultural conflicts that were underway in the streets and neighbourhoods of North India and in the context of municipal politics. And then, in some years, it ceased to engage with its Muslim critics altogether and unilaterally termed itself the sole representative of the Indian nation. A sweeping claim like this could always invite an equally seeping counterclaim. As it happened, within years, numbers of very prominent Indo-Muslim elites organised themselves and approached the colonial establishment claiming to be representing Indian Muslims at large. Soon after, the AIML emerged as an institutional expression of this position. When the Congress substantively engaged with the AIML, it again ended up conceding too much. The 'Lucknow Pact' that the Congress and the AIML signed granted Muslims 'weightage' in provinces in which they were in a minority. Though this was in lieu of the AIML accepting Muslims being underrepresented in Bengal and Punjab, both Muslim-majority provinces, the Pact sure legitimised the notion that Muslims could seek and receive political representation in excess of their share in the population of India. This perhaps boosted Muslim expectations regarding political representation beyond logical containment. Especially since, earlier, the reforms of 1909 had granted the Muslims 'weightage' too along with a separate electorate. The Nehru Report, an informal constitution of sorts drafted by Motilal Nehru in 1928, did try to reverse these concessions. It rejected the principle of communal electorates and recommended reserved seats for Muslims at the centre and only in the provinces in which they were in a minority.[28] But, perhaps, this seeming attempt by the Congress to set logical limits to the discourse around Muslim political presentation came rather too late. Surveying the politics of colonial India, one is tempted to think that Jinnah's demand for political parity between Hindus and Muslims was a natural outcome of the 'weightage' the Congress had originally conceded to the Muslims in 1916. Parity, after all, is but exaggerated 'weightage'. The root cause of partition, one might say, was that this was just too unreasonable a demand to be legitimately considered. The origins of Pakistan sure owed a bit to the Congress's missteps. The Congress, in this sense, was a part of the seedbed from which Pakistan emerged.

---

28 See Bipan Chandra, et. al, *India's Struggle for Independence* (Penguin Books, 1989), p.263.

APPENDIX

Muslim Participation in the Annual Congresses. 1885-1906

Year	Total Number of Delegates	Number of Muslim Delegates*	Percentage of Muslim Delegates
1885	72	2	2.77
1886	434	32	7.37
1887	606	65	10.72
1888	1248	209	16.74
1889	1889	237	12.54
1890	677	116	17.13
1891*	-	-	-
1892	625	75	12.0
1893	867	59	6.80
1894	1163	22	1.89
1895	1584	20	1.26
1896	784	53	6.76
1897	692	47	6.69
1898	611	6	0.98
1899	789	306	38.78
1900	567	50	8.81
1901	896	74	8.25
1902	471	16	3.39
1903	538	9	1.67
1904	1010	35	3.46
1905	757	16	2.11
1906	1663	45	2.70

* I counted the obviously Muslim sounding names in the delegate lists to arrive at the figure of Muslim delegates for a year.

* The delegate list of the year was illegible due to bad microfilming.

Source: *Indian National Congress Proceedings, National Archives of India, Microfilm Nos. 1433-35.*

BIBLIOGRAPHY

PRIMARY SOURCES

Badruddin Tyabji Papers, National Archives of India, New Delhi, Microfilm Nos. 1333-35

Bengalee (newspaper), Nehru Memorial Museum and Library, New Delhi, Microfilm No. 1042

Indian National Congress Proceedings, National Archives of India, New Delhi, Microfilm Nos. 1433-35

Malik, Hafeez, ed., *Political Profile of Syed Ahmed Khan. A Documentary Record* (New Delhi: Adam Publishers and Distributers, 2006)

Mohammad, Shan, ed., *The Aligarh Movement: Basic Documents. 1864-1898. Vol. III* (Meerut, New Delhi: Meenakshi Prakashan)

_________________, ed., *Writings and Speeches of Syed Ahmad Khan* (Bombay: Nachiketa Publications Limited, 1972)

Pirzada, Syed Sharifuddin, ed., *Foundations of Pakistan. All-India Muslim League Documents. 1906-1947. Vol. II. 1924-1947*

(Karachi, Dacca: National Publishing House, 1970)

Zaidi, A.M. and Zaidi, S., eds., *The Encyclopedia of the Indian National Congress, Vol. I, 1885-1890, The Founding Fathers* (New Delhi: S. Chand & Company Ltd., 1976)

______________________, eds., *The Encyclopaedia of the Indian National Congress. Volume Three: 1896-1900. Gathering Storms* (New Delhi: S. Chand & Company Ltd., 1977)

SECONDARY SOURCES

Articles and Book Chapters

Barrier, N. Gerald, 'The Punjab Government and Communal Politics,' *The Journal of Asian Studies*, Vol. 27, No. 3 (May, 1968)

Bayly, C.A., 'Local Control in Indian Towns – The Case of Allahabad. 1880-1920,' *Modern Asian Studies*. Vol. 5, No. 4 (1971)

___________., 'Returning the British to South Asian History: The Limits of Colonial Hegemony,' *Origins of Nationality in South Asia: Patriotism and Ethical Government in the Making of Modern India* (New Delhi: OUP, 2001)

Freitag, Sandria, 'Contesting in Public: Colonial Legacy and Contemporary Communalism,' David Ludden, ed., *Contesting the Nation: Religion, Community, and the Politics of Democracy in India* (Philadelphia: University of Pennsylvania Press, 1996)

Hasan, Mushirul, 'Sharif Culture and Colonial Rule: A *Maulvi*-Missionary Encounter,' Mushirul Hasan and Asim Roy, eds., *Living Together Separately. Cultural India in History and Politics* (New Delhi: OUP, 2005)

Hasan, S. Nurul, 'Aspects of State and Religion in Medieval India' and 'Shaikh Ahmad Sirhindi and Mughal Politics,' Satish Chandra, ed., *Religion, State, and Society in Medieval India. Collected Works of S. Nurul Hasan* (New Delhi: OUP,2005)

Kurin, Richard, 'The Culture of Ethnicity in Pakistan,' Katherine P. Ewing, ed., *Shariat and Ambiguity in South Asian* Islam, Berkeley: University of California Press, 1988)

Pollock, Sheldon, 'Ramayana and the Political Imagination in India,' *The Journal of Asian* Studies, Vol. 52, No. 2 (May, 1993)

Robinson, Francis, 'Islam and Muslim Separatism,' *Islam and Muslim History in South Asia* (New Delhi: OUP, 2000)

________________, 'Islamic Reform and Modernities in South Asia,' *Modern Asian Studies,* Vol.42, NO. 2/3, Islam in South Asia (Mar.-May, 2008)

________________, 'Living Together Separately: The '*Ulama* of Farangi Mahall. *C.* 1700 – *C.* 1950,' Mushirul Hasan and Asim Roy, eds., *Living Together Separately. Cultural India in History and Politics* (New Delhi: OUP, 2005)

________________, 'Municipal Government and Muslim Separatism in the United Provinces. 1883 to 1916,' *Modern Asian Studies.* Vol. 7, No. 3 (1973)

________________, 'Nation-formation: The Brass Thesis and Muslim Separatism,' *Islam and Muslim History in South Asia* (New Delhi: OUP, 2000)

________________, 'Perso-Islamic Culture in India from the Seventeenth to the Early Twentieth Century,' *The 'Ulama' of Farangi Mahall and Islamic Culture in South Asia* (Permanent Black, 2001)

Shaikh, Farzana, 'Muslims and Political Representation in Colonial India: The Making of Pakistan,' *Modern Asian Studies*, 1986, Vol. 20, No. 3 (1986)

BOOKS

Abbasi, Mohammad Yusuf, *The Genesis of Muslim Fundamentalism in British India* (Publication Department: Indian Institute of Applied Political Research, 1987)

Ahmad, Aziz, *An Intellectual History of Islam in India* (Edinburgh University Press, 1969)

Ahmed, Rafiuddin, *The Bengal Muslims. A Quest for Identity. 1871-906* (Delhi: OUP, 1981)

Alam, Muzaffar, *The Languages of Political Islam in India* (Delhi: Ashoka University in association with Permanent Black, 2016 [Fourth Paperback Impression])

Ali, M. Athar, *The Mughal Nobility Under Aurangzeb* (New Delhi: OUP, 2001)

__________________, *Mughal India. Studies in Polity, Ideas, Society and Culture* (New Delhi: OUP, 2008)

Appadorai, A., *The Substance of Politics* (New Delhi: OUP, 2020 [Twenty-Seventh Impression])

Bandyopadhyay, Sekhar, *From Plassey to Partition and After. A History of Modern India* (Hyderabad: Orient BlackSwan, 2022 [Second Edition])

Barraclough, G., *The Origins of Modern Germany* (New York, London: W.W. Norton & Company, 1984)

Bayly, C.A., *Rulers, Townsmen and Bazaars. North Indian Society in the Age of British Expansion. 1770-1870* (OUP: New Delhi, 2014 [Second Impression])

Brass, Paul R., *Language, Religion and Politics in North* India (Delhi: Vikas Publishing House, 1975)

Brown, Judith M., *Modern India. The Origins of an Asian*

Democracy (OUP, 1994)

Chandra, Bipan, et. al, *India's Struggle for Independence* (Penguin Books, 1989)

Chandra, Satish, *Essays on Medieval Indian History* (New Delhi: OUP, 2005)

__________, *Medieval India. From the Sultanat to the Mughals. Part Two (1526-1748)* (New Delhi: Har-Anand Publications, 2000)

__________, *State, Society, and Culture in Indian History* (New Delhi: OUP, 2012)

Chatterji, Joya, *Bengal Divided. Hindu Communalism and Partition, 1932-1947* (CUP:1994)

Chopra, P.N., Gopal, Ram, and Bhargava, M.L., *A Century of the Indian National Congress. 1885-1985* (Delhi: Agam Prakashan, 1986)

Cohn, B.S., *Colonialism and Forms of Knowledge. The British in India* (Princeton, New Jersey: Princeton University Press, 1996)

Deepak, J. Sai, *India that is Bharat. Coloniality, Civilisation, Constitution* (New Delhi: Bloomsbury, 2021)

Dhulipala, Venkat, *Creating a New Medina. State Power, Islam, and the Quest for Pakistan in Late Colonial North India* (New Delhi: CUP, 2017)

Dirks, Nicholas B., *Castes of Mind. Colonialism and the Making of Modern India* (Delhi: Permanent Black, 2016 [Ninth Impression])

__________, *The Hollow Crown. Ethnohistory of an Indian Kingdom* (Cambridge, New York, New Rochelle, Melbourne, Sydney: CUP, 2008)

Eaton, Richard M., *India in the Persianate Age* (Allen Lane, an Imprint of Penguin Books, 2019)

______________, *Temple Desecration and Muslim States in Medieval India* (New Delhi: Hope India, 2004)

______________, *Essays on Islam and Indian History* (New Delhi: OUP, 2000)

Foucault, Michel, *Power. Essential Works. 1954-84. Volume Three* (Penguin Random House, 1994)

______________, *The Archeology of Knowledge* (Routledge, 2009)

Freitag, Sandria B., *Collective Action and Community. Public Arenas and Emergence of Communalism in North India* (New Delhi: OUP, 1990)

Geertz, Clifford, *The Interpretation of Cultures* (New York: Basic Books, 1973)

Gellner, Ernest, *Nations and Nationalism* (Ithaca, New York: Cornell University Press, 2006)

Gilmartin, David, *Empire and Islam. Punjab and the Making of Pakistan* (Delhi, Bombay, Calcutta, Madras: OUP, 1989)

Gopal, Ram, *Indian Muslims. A Political History. 1858-1947* (Bomaby, Calcutta, New Delhi, Madras, London, New York: Asia Publishing House, 1959)

Habib, Irfan, *The Agrarian System of Mughal India* (New Delhi: OUP, 1999)

Hardy, Peter, *The Muslims of British India* (CUP, 1998)

Hasan, Mushirul, *A Moral Reckoning. Muslim Intellectuals in Nineteenth Century Delhi* (New Delhi: OUP, 2005)

______________, *From Pluralism to Separatism. Qasbas in Colonial Awadh* (New Delhi: OUP, 2012 [Second Impression])

______________, *Nationalism and Communal Politics in India,*

1885-1930 (New Delhi: Manohar, 2000)

Heimsath, Charles H., *Indian Nationalism and Hindu Social Reform*, (OUP, 1964)

Hobsbawm, Eric, *Nations and Nationalism since 1780* (CUP, 2012 [Second Edition])

Hodgson, Marshal G. S., *The Venture of Islam. Conscience and History in a World Civilization. Vol. 1, The Classical Age of Islam* (Chicago and London: The University of Chicago Press, 1977)

Huntington, Samuel P., *The Clash of Civilizations and the Remaking of World Order* (Penguin Books, 2016)

Jain, Meenakshi, *Flight of Deities and Rebirth of Temples* (New Delhi: Aryan Books International, 2019)

Jalal, Ayesha, *Self and Sovereignty. Individual and Community in South Asia Islam Since 1850* (New Delhi: OUP, 2001)

___________, *The Sole Spokesman. Jinnah, the Muslim League and the Demand for Pakistan* (CUP, 2017).

Jones, Kenneth, *Arya Dharma: Hindu Consciousness in 19th-Century Punjab* (New Delhi: Manohar, 1989)

Joshi, Shashi and Josh, Bhagwan, *Struggle for Hegemony in India, Vol. 3, Culture Community and Power* (New Delhi: Sage Publications, 1994)

King, Christopher R., *One Language Two Scripts. The Hindi Movement in Nineteenth Century North India* (Bombay: OUP, 1994)

Kulikowski, Michael, *The Triumph of Rome. The Roman World from Hadrian to Constantine* (Cambridge, Massachusetts: Harvard University Press, 2016)

Kulke, Hermann, ed., *The State in India. 1000-1700* (New Delhi:

OUP, 2004 [Third Impression])

Kumar, Sunil, *The Emergence of the Delhi Sultanate* (Permanent Black in association with Ashoka University, 2007)

Lelyveld, David, *Aligarh's First Generation. Muslim Solidarity in British India* (New Delhi: OUP, 1996)

MacCulloch, Diarmaid, *Christianity. The First Three Thousand Years* (Penguin Books, 2009)

McLane, John R., *Indian Nationalism and the Early Congress,* (Princeton University Press, 1977)

Mehrotra, S.R , *A History of the Indian National Congress,* Vol. I, 1885-1918 (Delhi: Vikas Publishing House, 1995)

Metcalf, Barbara Dally, *Islamic Revival in British India, 1860-1900* (Karachi: Royal Book Company, 1989)

Mody, Homy, *Sir Pherozeshah Mehta: A Political Biography* (Delhi: Asia Publishing House, 1963), p. 100.

Mujeeb, M., *The Indian Muslims* (New Delhi: Munshiram Manoharlal Publishers Pvt. Ltd., 2017 [Fourth Reprint])

Pandey, Gyanendra, *The Construction of Communalism in Colonial North India* (New Delhi: OUP, Oxford India Perennials, 2012 [Third Edition])

Pollock, Sheldon, *The Language of the Gods in the World of Men. Sanskrit, Culture and Power in Premodern India* (Ranikhet: Permanent Black, 2007 [Third Impression])

Rai, Alok, *Hindi Nationalism* (Hyderabad: Orient BlackSwan, 2001 [Reprinted 2002, 2007, 2018])

Rai, Amrit, *A House Divided. The Origin and Development of Hindi/ Hindavi* (Delhi: OUP, 1984)

Rizvi, S.A.A., *The Wonder that was India II* (Picador India, 2018)

Robinson, Francis, *Separatism Among Indian Muslims. The Politics of the United Provinces' Muslims. 1860-*1923 (New Delhi: OUP, 1994 [Second Impression])

Sarkar, Sumit, *Modern India. 1885-1947* (New Delhi: Macmillan India Ltd., 1983)

Sharma, Ram Sharan, *Aspects of Political Ideas and Institutions in Ancient India* (Delhi: Motilal Banarasidas Publishers Private Limited, 1999)

Sheikh, Farzana, *Community and Consensus in Islam. Muslim representation in Colonial India. 1860-1947* (Melbourne: CUP, 1989)

Singh, Anita Inder, *The Origins of the Partition of India. 1936-47* (Bombay, Calcutta, Madras: OUP, 1990)

Smith, Wilfred Cantwell, *Modern Islam in India. A Social Analysis* (London: Victor Gollancz Ltd., 1946)

Stein, Burton, *Peasant State and Society in Medieval South India* (Delhi: OUP, 1980)

Thapar, Romila, *From Lineage to State. Social Formations in the Mid-First Millennium B.C. in the Ganga Valley* (New Delhi: OUP, 2000 [Sixth Impression])

Tombs, Robert, *The English and their History* (Penguin Books, 2014)

Trevelyan, G.M., *A Shortened History of England* (Penguin Books)

Wells, Colin, *The Roman Empire* (Fontana Press, 1992 [Second Edition])